IN HIS IMAGE

IN HIS IMAGE

Understanding and Embracing the Poor

Andy Matheson

Authentic

16 15 14 13 12 11 10   7 6 5 4 3 2 1

First published 2010 by Authentic Media Limited
Milton Keynes
www.authenticmedia.co.uk

British Library Cataloguing in Publication Data

A catalogue record for this book is available from the
British Library

ISBN-13: 978-1-85078-870-6

Authentic publishes Christian books to help all Christians, wherever they are
on their spiritual journey. the publishers do not necessarily agree with every
view communicated by the authors, or with every interpretation of Scripture
expressed. We leave readers to come to their own conclusions in the light of
their understanding of God's Word and in an attitude of Christian love and
fellowship.

Cover design by Phil Houghton
Cover photograph by Nick Catling and Carl Bowen
Printed and bound in Great Britain by Cox and Wyman, Reading

CONTENTS

To my family – Joan, Claire, Lisa and Jamie
who have shared so much of the journey
contained in this book and have been the
best companions I could have hoped for
along the way

Acknowledgements

There are many people I would like to thank for helping me through the process of writing this book.

A number of people working with Oasis around the world helped to compile material. Thank you Flora, Charles, Divya, Susie, Chantel, Thobe, Kate, Carol, Jo, Dave, Accamma, Kuldeep, Ruth, Jenny, Cathy, Anita, Laura, Jeanie and Phil.

A big thank you also to Chris Mungeam, who suggested I write in the first place and then helped in so many ways as I explored the uncharted territory of publishing. Thank you also to Rebecca Halfacre, Lydia Fry, Margaret Lock, Joan Matheson and Tara Smith, who assisted at various points with the editing process.

I am really grateful to Bob Moffett, Andrew and James Perry, Pete Brierley and Graham Mungeam, for reading through the material and giving such insightful feedback as the manuscript began to take shape. Your comments have been invaluable.

Introduction

I recently saw a great five-minute film on the Internet called 'Chicken à la Carte'. It shows two Asian girls eating their fast-food chicken, but then it follows the path of the leftovers as they are collected up and taken in bags and bins to feed children and families on the edge of town. It makes the point that hunger is a major reality in our day. It also makes the point that those who 'have' in abundance often take what they have for granted, whereas those who 'don't have' are often extremely grateful for the scraps they get. Subtler still is the message that we live in a connected world – that what some of us discard others may eat.

I've never met the film's creator and producer, Ferdinand Dimadura. What I do know from watching his short film, though, is that he wants to bring about change in our world. He wants inequality and injustice to be overturned. And it is brilliant to see the momentum that has been generated in the past few years for a more equitable and just world. Among those advocating for this change are many followers of Jesus. People have been working for this kind of change for a long time, of course, but in recent years there seem to be so many more people who won't settle for injustice; who won't bury their heads in the sand and ignore their neighbours both locally and globally; who refuse to become cocooned in the safety of their church community and ignore the plight of the poor. It is very encouraging. You may be one of those people – and, if you are, I hope this book will help you in some small way in that task. If you are not, I hope that reading this book will inspire you to join with the thousands of others who are already engaged in some way in helping the poor.

This book is, in part, about my personal journey trying to understand how we should engage among the poor. For that reason, these pages contain many stories of how I, along with those who also work or worked for Oasis, witnessed what God was doing in and through and among us.[1] The team we had in India when we began working there, and the teams around the world today, are made up of wonderful people whom I admire greatly. What I learned and share with you in this book did not happen in isolation but in the community of people among and with whom we worked.

The years since we left India have allowed me to try to make the important connections between theological truth, principles of effective engagement and life experience. Many people outside Oasis have also played a key role in my learning and development, and their impact undergirds much of the material in the following pages. Some of these I have met only through their writings, which have had a profound impact on me. Still others have mentored me, given me timely advice and encouragement, and have been more important to me than any of them could have imagined.

This is not a book of definitive answers. Rather, it explores issues connected to work among the poor and offers principles of engagement rather than prescriptive approaches. Because we don't have all the answers, and because a solution in one situation doesn't necessarily work in another, we have to continually seek God's wisdom and understanding - not our own. And so while the principles contained in this book are applicable in many contexts and situations, they must always be employed in the context of prayer and openness to God.

I hope that the stories in this book will not only illustrate and explain the concepts and principles, but that they will also bring these experiences to life. My experiences among the poor have inspired me to look at Scripture afresh, through a new lens, to discover truth. I have learned so much from this dynamic as I have gone back and forth between real-life engagement and Scripture. The principles that follow, therefore, are rooted in biblical truth that is also applicable to real-life experience.

In focusing on this one key belief, that 'all people are made in the image of God', I want to make clear at the beginning that I am not disregarding other truths of Scripture which are also important. I do not dispute the fact or the consequences of what we traditionally call 'the fall'. I believe that when sin entered the world it had a profound impact on each individual and every community and that its reach was indeed global. I believe that sin impacts individual people but that it also impacts the ways we relate to one another. Sin's effects are systemic as well as personal. But I focus on this truth that we often neglect, that 'all people are made in the likeness of God', because I believe this to be the starting point when we engage among the poor. In doing so I am not disregarding the clear understanding of Scripture that we are all sinners and in need of God's grace and mercy.

How we view poverty will directly impact how we engage among the poor. If poverty, as we will be suggesting, is multidimensional and encompasses material possessions, marginalization, injustice, exploitation, and much, much more, then our approach with both individuals and communities that are poor needs to be multidimensional as well. To think that we should simply preach the gospel or simply provide food and clothing or just help people find work is naïve. Our approach needs to be not only multidimensional but also integrated.

The first two chapters lay the foundation for the rest of the book. Chapter 1 discusses what it means to be made in God's image and Chapter 2 then develops a framework for understanding poverty. The rest of the book focuses on relating these principles to how we engage among those who are poor, both individuals and communities. The approach we take – our framework of reference – is crucial if we are to be effective in helping those who are disadvantaged. As we apply these fundamental truths to our work – that all people are made in God's image and that poverty is multidimensional in nature – we will gain new insight into the predicament of the poor. We will appreciate God's unending love for them in new and deeper ways as we also explore who God calls us to be and what God calls us to do.

1

Made in God's Image

The ultimate test of our relationship with God is in how we react to our fellow human beings who are created in his image, especially those in need.

– Chick Yuill[1]

Ruth grew up in a poor family in a village in Zimbabwe. When she was about five years old, her father started abusing her sexually. Perhaps he abused her because of a belief, rooted in witchcraft, that this practice would make his business more profitable. Ruth told her mother about the abuse, but she was either powerless to do anything or chose not to intervene. When she was about ten years old Ruth ran away from home but was raped by the conductor of the bus she caught to take her to the city. The conductor was caught by a policeman, who arrested him, and the conductor was later convicted in court.

About three years later, while on the streets, Ruth was raped again – this time by a man who professed to be a witch hunter. He was not convicted because the crime was never reported to the police. When she was fifteen Ruth was hired to work as a housemaid for a family. The wife was often away, leaving Ruth in the house with the father and the children. In February 2004 this man raped her a number of times and she eventually reported him to the police. Since Ruth had had little education, when he produced a piece of paper for her to sign she didn't realize that it was an affidavit saying they were lovers. She became pregnant as a result of the rape and was thrown out of the house. It was at that point that she was put in touch with our Oasis team in Harare. We followed through with the charge of rape, maintaining that Ruth had signed the affidavit under coercion. But, because she didn't have a birth certificate, the court accepted the man's claim that he had thought she was twenty-five years old. He escaped prosecution.

All of us would agree that Ruth's story is heartbreaking but, if you could meet Ruth, what would you want to convey to her? Many Christians have traditionally taken sin as their starting point in such conversations. The crucial thing for people to understand (they have reasoned), is our alienation from God, who is perfect, and our need to confess and receive God's forgiveness. But is that really the best starting point? When someone has suffered as deeply as Ruth has, introducing her to God by emphasizing her personal responsibility before God would probably only lead to further shame and guilt. But even if Ruth was personally responsible for her own predicament, even if she was homeless because of poor choices she had made, is a message about her sinful state before a holy God really what she needs to hear first? I don't think so.

Instead, I propose that our starting point when we meet those like Ruth and the millions of others she represents – the poor, oppressed, alienated, and disadvantaged in our society – is actually a different place. I propose we begin by affirming their capacity for goodness, compassion, perseverance, and love. I try to do that with my own children. Instead of pointing out their failures, which is so easy to do, I try to focus on the goodness each of them displays. This doesn't always come naturally. When I coach my daughter in tennis, I have a couple of choices. I can either point out every time she doesn't throw the ball high enough on her serve, or swings at her volleys, *or* I can shout 'Yes, great!' every time she does it correctly and hits a good shot. I try to take the latter approach more often than the former because I know it makes the greatest difference.

There is a biblical precedent for this starting point. After all, Genesis 1 comes before Genesis 3. People are made in the image of God before sin comes into the world. In fact, the fall in Genesis 3 is so horrendous because our creation in God's image in Genesis 1 is so wonderful. The two are linked.[2] And even though the fall marred and scarred God's image in us, it still remains and can still be seen. However broken a person becomes through the trauma of life, God's image in them remains. To be made in the image of God is to be human. Original goodness existed before original sin.

The fact that God made *all people* in his image provides us with a framework as we follow Jesus to seek out those who are poor and marginalized in our society. This truth helps us understand what poverty is all about, how we should approach the poor, and how 'those who are poor in the eyes of the world' can also be 'rich in faith'.[3] Evangelists often comment on the fact that at the foot of the cross the ground is even. Everyone who stands there is on an equal footing with the rest of humanity, for 'all have sinned and fall short of the glory of God'.[4] In the same way, we all reflect God's image, and in equal measure. Regardless of what we do or what others do to us, God's image remains in us. No person who has been born possesses the image of God in greater measure than anyone else – Jew and Gentile, slave and free, man and woman is how the Bible puts it. We might add Iraqi and

American, Muslim and atheist, liberal and conservative, rich and poor. God created them *all* in his image, and we should treat them *all* as equals. This is foundational for understanding equity, equality and justice. It is also foundational for understanding the worth of every human being. As Jesus pointed out as he talked of God's common grace, 'Look at the birds of the air; they do not sow or reap or store away in barns, and yet your heavenly Father feeds them. Are you not much more valuable than they?'[5] The unspoken contrast here, of course, is that although God created the birds of the air, God did not make them in his image. But the fact that God has made each and every human being in his image is the basis for their incredible value. Therefore we need to treat *all* people with dignity. When people ignore the poor, hoping they will go away, or when they work among the poor in a patronizing way, they fail to acknowledge the value that God ascribes to all people and in doing so demonstrate a failure to understand this core theological truth.

Although theologians differ widely in their interpretations of this doctrine of the image of God,[6] this chapter focuses on a few foundational truths that will enable us to apply an understanding of God's image to work among the poor. Genesis 1 in particular, as we will see, both states and implies some of these important truths.

The Image of God Is Fundamental to Personhood

Being made in the image of God is intrinsic to who we are. Derek Kidner makes this abundantly clear when he says, 'As long as we are human we are, by definition, in the image of God.'[7] God did not create Adam and Eve and then add the component we describe as 'his image' afterwards. By definition, a person is made in God's image. And, as we have said, sin has no power to erase God's image in a person – not the sins of an individual, the sins of others that affect that individual, or the sin of the world. Ray Anderson makes clear that God's image is an integral part of who we are and how we live as human beings.

> Being in the image of God is not a religious overlay on our natural humanity. On the contrary, being in the image of God is itself fundamental to our true humanity. Without the freedom to be for God and the other, we are living in contradiction to our basic humanity. To live in such a way as to resist the Word and will of God in favor of our own instinctive rights and desires is to live inhumanly, not just nonreligiously.[8]

Chris Wright points out that the term 'in our image' is not an adjectival phrase but an adverbial one. It reflects, therefore, more about the way God made us and who God made us to be than any of our characteristics or qualities. As Wright says, 'The image of God is not so much something we possess, as what we are. To be human is to be the image of God. It is not an extra added on to our species: it is definitive of what it means to be human.'[9]

Both Body and Soul Reflect the Image of God

If we begin to think of God's image as being reflected in only one aspect of our humanness, we create a dualism that cannot be substantiated biblically. One result of such dualism[10] can be to disregard the body as being less important than the soul. That focus on the soul can, in turn, lead us to a 'disregard of the personal existence of others in their embodied form'.[11] As Ray Anderson says,

From a biblical perspective, no fundamental distinction can be made between the human person as an embodied soul and as an ensouled body. Consequently, we conclude that the imago Dei is borne as a concrete and particular endowment of each person's existence as embodied personal being.[12]

Gerhard von Rad makes a similar point in his commentary on Genesis.

The interpretations, therefore, are to be rejected which proceed from an anthropology strange to the Old Testament and one-sidedly limit God's image to man's spiritual nature, relating it to man's 'dignity,' his 'personality' or 'ability for moral decision,' etc. The marvel of man's bodily appearance is not at all to be excepted from the realm of God's image.[13]

If it were true that the image of God is reflected in a person's soul and not their body, then one would expect Scripture to give far less emphasis to people's physical needs. But Jesus spends as much time helping people with bodily sickness as he does helping them with spiritual sickness. This understanding that God's image is the essence of our total humanness leads us to a holistic concern for all people.[14] Chris Wright emphasizes this point when he says that the Genesis 2:7 reference to the human person as a 'living being' includes the physical, spiritual, rational and social dimensions of personhood.[15]

The Entry of Sin into the World Affects the Image of God in People

Sin's entrance into the world had an impact on every dimension of personhood and life. While some theologians use terms like 'total depravity' in talking about this impact, I don't think it is a helpful phrase. Others have pointed to the issue of guilt as fundamental because the primary impact of the fall was to separate human beings from God. G.C. Berkouwer says that 'Living his life within the limits of his common humanity, man is arraigned by Scripture as guilty before God. For he is alienated from God's glory in this humanness given him by God.'[16] Certainly sin has negatively affected humankind in all of our relationships, and relationships are central to personhood because they reflect God's nature. One aspect of being made in God's image is the fact that we are relational. Later on we will relate this to our understanding of poverty. Just as we cannot precisely define the nature of the image of God, neither can we detail the nature of the fall's impact on that image. Certainly we see evidence in Scripture and in our lives that sin, both individual and corporate, has marred and scarred the image of God in all people. According to Alan Richardson, 'The biblical position can best be summarized by saying that the divine image is defaced but not obliterated at the fall (or by man's sin).'[17]

The Image Remains after the Fall

Some have argued that the fall obliterated the image of God in people. But those who have tried to do so find it difficult to explain the fact that Genesis 5:1–2, which traces history from Adam to Noah, many generations after the fall, reiterates the original statement that Adam and Eve were made in the likeness of God. And again a few chapters later, in the context of his covenant with Noah, God reminds him of his responsibility for his fellow human beings saying, 'for in the image of God has God made all people'.[18] Here God links the fact that people are made in his image to the prohibition against murder. The fact that this took place after the fall is   another indication that the image of God was not obliterated at the time of the fall. As Anthony Hoekema reminds us,

> We may indeed think of the image of God as having been tarnished through man's fall into sin, but to affirm that man had by this time completely lost the image of God is to affirm something that the sacred text does not say.[19]

Ray Anderson has pointed out that Jesus' statement that hatred for another person is like murder is based on this same understanding – other creaturely beings do not share the image of God, whereas all of humanity does.[20] It appears that, in Jesus' view, the image of God was still present in all people.

The Terms 'Image' and 'Likeness' Are Complementary

Others have argued that the terms 'image' and 'likeness', both found in the Genesis 1 narrative, indicate two separate aspects of humanity. While one of these remains (these theologians have posited), the other was obliterated because of the fall. This argument, however, is built upon a misunderstanding of the Hebrew terms. As many scholars, including Doug Baker, have pointed out, these two terms are in fact complementary.

> They amplify each other rather than referring to two different things. The use of the two words reflects the fact that a full and pregnant idea is being expressed, and to use only a single word, even if it fulfilled the meaning, would leave an emotional void. The Bible is replete with this literary device

of pairing words and ideas, especially in the Old Testament, and the effect is to increase the emotional impact and the urgency of the message, as well as to sharpen the focus on the subject.[21]

The fact that the two terms are used interchangeably in the passages mentioned above further supports this idea that they emphasize the importance of a single concept. Genesis 5:1 uses the term likeness (*demuth*), while Genesis 9:6 uses the word image (*tselem*). In neither context is there any indication that these words refer only to an aspect of an individual and not to the whole person.[22]

Imaging God as a Mandate

In Doug Baker's stimulating book on the subject he argues that there are linguistic reasons why we are to understand 'in our image' not as indicating inherent qualities but rather as the mandate that God is giving to humankind. We are to reflect, or 'image', God in the world. 'We were to mirror God's glory to each other, to all creation, and especially to God himself. This mandate encompasses our entire person, our entire race, all aspects of our lives, all of our history, and even all of our future.'[23] Such an understanding is in contrast to the more traditional approach that has focused on the characteristics and qualities of humanity that reflect our understanding of God. The two, however, are not mutually exclusive. As Anthony Hoekema says, 'It is my conviction that we need to maintain both aspects. Since the image of God includes the whole person, it must include both man's structure and man's functioning.'[24]

Our mandate in stewarding God's world is a mandate to reflect God. If ever there was a high calling, surely that

is it. And all of us, as those made in his image, share this
call.

The Image of God Restored through Reconnection with God

Through our reconnection with the one who created
humankind, we all can be renewed – that is, transformed into the likeness of Christ. Such transformation
is available to all people and, when it occurs, it has a
profound impact on every aspect of our lives. Such
renewal is not simply about adding a spiritual dimension to our lives. It is about renewing our whole lives.
Paul talks about being renewed in God's image in his
letter to the church at Colosse when he says, 'Do not lie
to each other, since you have taken off your old self with
its practices and have put on the new self, which is
being renewed in knowledge in the image of its creator.'[25] G.C. Berkouwer, reflecting on this passage,
points out that Paul immediately goes on to talk about a
new community where people, though they remain
with their differences, are able to become a new community. A new community is not possible because these
differences are removed, he says; rather, it is possible
precisely because of these differences. 'Thus', he says,
'when we consider the image of God in man as it is
restored in Christ, we are not concerned with some
"analogy" of ego or personality or self-consciousness,
but rather with the fullness of the new life, which can be
described as a new relationship with God, and in this
relationship as the reality of salvation.'[26]

If there is an arena of witness in the world that we can
be tempted to overlook, it is this one – the community of
the church. The church is characterized by people who

remain imperfect yet who, because of their reconnection with God, create a community that should be attractive and welcoming to everyone. Such a community is always a powerful witness to how God's image is restored in individual lives.

Conclusion

With a better perspective on what it means to be created in the image of God and to live in the light of that, let's return to Ruth. I asked you above what you would want to convey to her. I'd like to tell her that she has inestimable value; that she has done so well in life just to come through her trauma; that her perseverance in the face of abuse is a light in our dark world. I'd like to tell her that although I cannot comprehend her pain, I know that God holds it with her and that God is on her side. I'd like to tell her that her unborn child is a gift, that she need not fear, that we are here for her too.

And, in fact, that is exactly what our staff in Harare conveyed to her – not just when she first arrived, but repeatedly over the following year and a half. We told her in words, and we told her in actions as we walked alongside her. Slowly she began to rebuild her life. She was very good with her hands, so she used to cut people's hair and charge them for it. With the money sometimes she would go and buy a sausage because that is what she wanted, but most of the time she saved the money for her baby who was on the way. She completed a course in embroidery and was by far the best student in her class. She was so talented, in fact, that the embroidery teacher, who ran an interior design business, hired her to embroider products for her clients. Ruth came to know Jesus and to trust God for her life. She was endowed with the tiniest soprano voice ever heard and she'd keep everyone laughing as she joked around. She would often say, 'My skin has become so smooth, it's like I have been bathing in milk.' She loved to sing – totally out of tune, but she loved to sing nonetheless. She was determined to become the best hairdresser and to one day open her own hairdressing place. We all believed that this would happen.

On the 19th of October 2006 Ruth gave birth to a baby girl and called her 'Tanaka', which means 'we did not have before but now we have in abundance and we occupy a place of honour'. In January 2005 her father died. In that same month Ruth tested positive for HIV. Over the course of that year she suffered much, always falling to opportunistic infections and struggling to come to terms with what might happen to her and the implications for her daughter. She was part of a support group, and these people continued to pray with her and encourage her while she questioned God. On the 9th of December our staff went to collect her mother because Ruth was asking for her. On the 15th of December her mother said she wanted to take her home, so she went home and on the 22nd of December she died. She was seventeen years old. I am glad that in those few months she came to know that God was on her side.

2

Understanding Poverty

Poverty is the absence of shalom in all its meanings.
– Bryant Myers[1]

Not long after arriving in Mumbai, our family got to know Sushila because she came to work in our home. Over time her story unfolded. She was the third of three daughters and grew up in a village in India. This village, where everyone knew everyone else and where timeless traditions still held sway over new ways of doing things, was very different from the urban context in which we first met Sushila. Although today the villages are changing, when she grew up technology meant a transistor radio and the occasional black and white TV. Some find village life to be a source of security. In Sushila's case, however, rejection by those closest to her, virtually no education, and her female status all meant that when she was married at fifteen and brought to the city, the scars already ran deep.

She began married life with renewed hope for the future, believing that finally she would experience the love she craved. It was not to be. As she adapted to the many challenges of life in this new environment she had the added burden of being expected to bear sons for her husband. He, of course, according to accepted cultural norms, was free of those same burdens that weigh so heavily on the other half of the human species. With minimal expectations as to how much he should contribute to his marriage and family life, he spent most of his time drinking and gambling. Not only did he fail to contribute to the family income, but he also wasted the money Sushila was able to earn. Sushila gave birth to two daughters, 19 months apart. A day or two after each delivery she was back working. A third daughter died at the age of eleven months. Eventually, in 1995, she gave birth to a son but he died within 24 hours.

Since Sushila was the only breadwinner, the family faced constant financial difficulties. Debts with local money-lenders, whose interest rates were exorbitant, built up over time. She'd had to take out a loan for an emergency medical need at the time of the death of her third child, and the payments were an ongoing pressure. She lived with the constant threat of retribution if she failed to make payments on time. Her husband would often drink too much and return home to beat her and her two daughters. Sushila was alone and desperate. She often contemplated dousing herself with kerosene and setting fire to herself, but concern for her daughters prevented her from taking such a step. On one occasion when things were particularly desperate she went so far as to pick up the kerosene bottle, only to find it miraculously empty. On another occasion her husband beat Sushila with a metal rod and threw her and her daughters out of the hutment. They spent the night huddled up outside. She was pregnant at the time, and she suffered heavy bleeding as a result.

For seven years we stood alongside Sushila as best we could. Since she helped us in our home, we saw her almost every day. She was honest, hardworking, faithful and generous. There were times of great joy in her life when she rose above her circumstances, and there were other times when God intervened in miraculous ways but, like so many in her situation, she lived from crisis to crisis. Her poverty was visible to the outside world by the fact that she lived in a corrugated tin hutment; walked to get water; held down six jobs at a time; and never went on holiday. But her poverty was much more than that. It had to do with the way she was treated by other people; the injustices she came to accept as normal; the way she was exploited; her inability to get out of her predicament regardless of how hard she worked.

There is certainly an economic dimension to poverty, but for many of the poor today the pain of their situation and circumstance runs much deeper than a lack of resources or possessions. It has to do with status, choice, opportunity, dignity, justice, relationship, community and hope. We will explore all of these aspects of poverty in subsequent chapters, but as we focus here on the fact that poverty is much broader than it is often understood to be, we begin with the economic dimensions to poverty.

Economic Dimensions to Poverty

When humankind was made in the image of God, God's blessings on them included children as well as the other resources God had created, which they were told to steward.[2] Animals, fish, plants and fruit trees were there for their benefit. The references in Genesis to humankind 'subduing' or 'having dominion over' the earth have sometimes been misinterpreted as a mandate for exploitation.[3] Fortunately, in recent times, many in the church worldwide have realized that this is not at all what the book of Genesis is saying. Humankind cert-ainly has work to do, which began with naming the animals, but 'subduing' and 'having dominion over' have to do with care and stewardship rather than exploitation. Adam and Eve had their first opportunities to 'image' God as they cared for the earth and everything that God had created.

All of the economic dimensions to poverty can be traced back to the misuse and exploitation of the earth and the failure of people to reflect God's image as they stewarded what he had provided. People first became economically poor not because there was not enough for all to live on but because stewardship was not exercised in the right way. The same is true today. If we were to steward our resources as a worldwide community properly, nobody today would go hungry. The problem is not that there isn't enough land or enough food but that we have forgotten that all people are made in God's image. In our greed and neglect we have failed to insist that there be an equitable system for acquiring and using the resources given by God. Dewi Hughes reminds us that,

> The central thrust of biblical teaching on economic activity is that everyone should enjoy the benefits that accrue from it. In this sphere Old Testament law, prophetic pronouncements and the teaching of Jesus and his apostles are very much biased towards the poor.[4]

We can see the stark inequity of the situation today in this single fact: the world's 497 billionaires are collectively worth $3.5 trillion, while the lowest income countries, made up of 2.4 billion people, are worth $1.6 trillion.[5] How could it all get so badly out of kilter? In the Western world, people sometimes justify such inequality by asserting our right to earn as much as we want. Ethics are, in this case, only applied to the process of creating wealth, and not to the extent of profit that a person can make. This reflects a type of capitalism that surely none of us would endorse. A biblical approach, of course, brings in the existence of God – who made *all* people in his image, who gave all people the task of being stewards of his good gifts, and who sought to preserve a measure of equality on the basis that all are tenants on his property and not owners. From that standpoint, the fact that anyone earns in the billions is obscene.

Rose lives on the ninth floor of a council house in London. She has four children aged between seven and fourteen, is a single mother, and does everything in her power to care for her family. She works round the clock to earn enough money for her children to have what they need. To say that this is exhausting is an understatement, but Rose always puts on a brave face and tries to look for the best in every situation. Day by day she is making a go of life, but when things go wrong it gets even tougher. Just recently the boiler stopped working and some of the doors in her small apartment broke. Her children didn't have any hot water or privacy, and the housing association where she lives wasn't interested in helping. It took three months for her boiler to be fixed and nobody has yet come to help with the doors. Ruth represents the millions of people in the UK and around the world who work hard, do what they can to get by and don't ask for charity. They could just do with a little extra of the $3.5 trillion owned by the wealthiest 497 people in the world.

The economic exploitation of the descendants of Abraham in Egypt was one part of their wider oppression. God saw this and, in response, sent Moses. Once the Israelites had been formed into a people, God made it clear that a community could live without economic exploitation and that a system of equity could be established – hence the whole series of laws that God gave to the people of Israel via Moses on Mount Sinai. By obeying these laws Israel could live as God's people in the land that they were about to enter. It is interesting that the land was both central to God's covenant with Israel and also the source of wealth for the people. And the key principle that God communicated regarding the land, which was to undergird how they lived as a community, was the principle of tenancy. 'The land must not be sold permanently, because the land is mine and you are but aliens and my tenants. Throughout the country that you hold as a possession, you must provide for the redemption of the land.'[6] Before they took possession of the land, God explained to them that their perspective must remain that of a tenant. They do not own God's creation, but they are stewards of it. Since God first introduced this principle of stewardship in the context of God's creation of humankind 'in his image', it may not be stretching it too far to say that it is one of the most important aspects of humankind's mirroring, reflecting or imaging God in our world. In other words, there is a crucial link in Scripture between economic poverty and stewardship – and a crucial link between stewardship and being made in God's image.

Alongside this understanding of tenancy was the principle of redemption of the land. This was a central aspect of the fiftieth year that God told them was to be a Jubilee.[7] One of the most amazing things about the concept of Jubilee is its practicality. People are going to become poor, but this is not a judgment upon them. Rather, instituting a system that provides periodic redistribution of the source of wealth gives the poor a chance to begin again and means that they will not remain poor forever. Poverty does not become a trap from which people cannot escape. Furthermore, if a person does become poor during the in-between time, God's people are to treat that person with special grace. God commanded that in those circumstances no interest of any kind was to be charged. And the motivation for such behaviour? The 'fear of God'.[8]

In fact, there were several laws that not only demonstrated special grace to those who had become poor but also ensured that their personal dignity was maintained. For example, those who became poor were not to be treated as slaves but as hired servants.[9] In another section God tells the people not to harvest every last piece of grain, but to allow the poor to glean from their fields, thereby giving them the opportunity to do something about their situation instead of relying on handouts. 'The gleanings that were left by the owner of a field or vineyard were not a handout but an opportunity for the poor. Like the owner the poor had to bring in the harvest if they were to benefit from the legislation.'[10] Personal dignity is as important for the poor person as it is for anyone else. We will return to explore this theme in more depth in Chapter 6.

God gave the principle of the 'year of Jubilee' to the entire people of Israel. In practice it would only help those who became poor if the whole community took responsibility for its implementation. The problem is that those who prosper and end up in control of the land not only have more to lose, but they also end up in positions of power. This power enables them to decide whether such a principle should direct their community or not. Justice for the poor is the responsibility of the entire community. We cannot think of poverty simply in individualistic terms, for the actions of one person always affect another. The laws of the land that seek to preserve justice are for all. When we are involved among the poor, we must remember that both the immediate community and the wider one can play a key role in either keeping people in a situation of poverty or releasing them from those chains that bind. In our globalized world, the community that impacts the poor extends across the globe.

Other Dimensions of Poverty

In one way, poverty is relative. I know people who think
of themselves as poor because they cannot afford the latest technology when everyone around them can.
Because in a consumerist society people measure life in
terms of what they possess, it is little wonder that some
view poverty as an absence of those things. But Scripture
does not view poverty in the same light – perhaps in part
because life in Palestine in Jesus' time was not materialistic in the same way we understand our own society to
be. In fact, when Jesus talked about the 'poor' he seemed
to refer to a much wider group of people characterized
not so much by how much they possessed but by their
relative marginalization within society. As Steve Chalke
and Alan Mann explain,

> Our narrow materialistic understanding of poverty stands
> in our way of grasping one of the major themes of the
> Sermon on the Mount, Jesus' teaching and the New
> Testament in general . . . For first-century Jews, the term
> poor was never limited to financial poverty. Rather, it could
> and did indicate social, spiritual, physical, political as well
> as financial exclusion, which were all interrelated.[11]

In Luke 4, Jesus' mandate to 'preach good news to the
poor' was fulfilled among those who were not necessarily economically poor but who were, for one reason or
another, on the margins of society. Tax collectors were a
case in point, and the wonderful description of Jesus'
encounter with Zacchaeus highlights a broader understanding of poverty in embracing a relational dynamic.
Tax collectors were despised by all. Not only were they
alienated from their fellow countrymen, but they were
also considered foreigners by the Romans whom they

served. They might have had bread on the table, but what does that matter if you have no friends to share it with? As Bryant Myers defines poverty,

> 'Poverty is a result of relationships that do not work, that are not just, that are not for life, that are not harmonious or enjoyable. Poverty is the absence of shalom in all its meanings.'[12]

Jesus also reached out to prostitutes – another group of people who might not have suffered for lack of food or clothing but who were ostracized and excluded and treated with contempt. Again, poverty for them was relational disempowerment rather than economic in nature. And when we understand this dimension of poverty we can appreciate the incident in Luke 7 at a deeper level. Here Jesus used a woman, most likely a prostitute, as an example of love in the presence of those who despised her. The context was a meal, this time in the home of Simon the Pharisee. It was customary at the time for religious leaders to invite a visiting speaker to a meal in their home and to share something that would prompt discussion. While the meal was in progress, a woman arrived at Jesus' feet. Picture Jesus, lying on his left side on a couch with a low table in front of him and his feet extended out towards the edge of the gathering. Others would also have been lying around the low table, almost in a circle. It was appropriate for those who were not invited to the meal to enter and watch, but they were not to eat or take part in discussion – and that is how this woman found a way to be at Jesus' feet.[13]

The woman began to weep and wet Jesus' feet with her tears. She wiped them with her hair and poured perfume over them. For some reason, Simon the host had failed to extend the basic gestures of hospitality to Jesus – and this woman, in a totally unexpected way, made up for his failing. How beautifully Luke tells us about the way Jesus then addressed Simon. He was not confrontational, but with care and compassion he looked at the woman and lifted her up as an example to all present. The one who has been forgiven much loves much. It is amazing to notice in this story that the woman never utters a word. She does not declare her need or invite Jesus to engage in conversation with her. Her actions speak from her heart and create a stark contrast with Simon's. And the simple parable that Jesus spoke, along with his words affirming this woman, opened the way for her to be perceived in a different light. Jesus urged those assembled in Simon's house, as he urges us today, not to disregard her as an outcast but to welcome her as a fellow traveller on the journey of life.

We will return to this theme of understanding marginalization and ostracism as key components of poverty in Chapter 3. And, in Chapter 10, we will examine in more depth how the poor teach us about faith and life as this woman does.

Poverty has many guises. While the immediate face of poverty is often economic, that is seldom the key issue. If you were to give $1,000 to a street child anywhere in the world, would that money rescue him or her from poverty? No. That money would provide the child and their friends with some great experiences, but it would last barely a week and then they would be back in the same situation they were in before. It is the mindset that people have that dictates their situation of poverty, more than the bank account they possess. If you gave that same $1,000 to someone in the bracket of 'working poor', someone who held down a job and who had some structure and discipline in their life, then that money would be used very differently. The working poor are not the same as the destitute poor[14] – their mindset is different and they would probably use the money well and not squander it. What makes this difference between the working and destitute poor? The working poor tend to live in community. They have relationships and they know what trust is, even if there are those who oppress them. The destitute poor don't live in community. They live fragmented lives dictated by their fragmented thoughts. They have no concern for tomorrow and they trust nobody. A large proportion of them suffer from mental illnesses.

For the working poor, it is often the lack of choice that is the debilitating factor. Somehow, however hard they work, they just can't seem to break through to a place where they have choices to make. They are caught in a trap from which they cannot escape unless someone helps them. This is why a woman becoming literate addresses issues of poverty. It is not that she has more income because she can read. But she sees the world differently and, as she does, she can begin to make choices that she didn't realize were hers to make. This is what happened to Shoba and Gita, two women who live in the Netaji Nagar slum in Mumbai. When our staff first met them they were disillusioned with life and constantly faced criticism from their wider families for a variety of reasons. Their respective spouses gave them no encouragement to study, but they both decided to enroll in the literacy classes that we were offering to women in that community. When they successfully completed the six-month course, a whole new world opened up to them. They were able to read the headlines in the local paper and sign their names to documents they could read instead of simply leaving a thumb impression. They have grown in confidence, and they are in the process of starting a small business and are helping other women in their community to learn to read and write.

The worst type of poverty, of course, is a poverty of hope. When people live day after day, year after year, without the resources to survive or opportunities to change their lives, sometimes it all just gets too much and hope evaporates. In India's slums this happens frequently. Women pour kerosene on themselves and light a match. It is an escape from the harsh reality of life for the millions who live with intolerable burdens and no hope. Suicide might be ethically wrong, but can you blame the woman who was married to an unemployed alcoholic who got himself into debt and then allowed his wife to face the wrath of the debt collectors when they came for their monthly payments at exorbitant interest rates? This was Sushila's plight, and it is the plight of so many others as well.

The Poor Will Always Be with Us

Occasionally, but thankfully not as often as was once the case, people will misuse the words of Jesus to ease their consciences about doing nothing for the millions of people who live in poverty. 'The poor you will always have with you'[15] has been used as a get-out clause by people who, for one reason or another, felt they could live their lives without due regard for those less fortunate than themselves. What Jesus said, in context, actually means the very opposite of what such people believe.

Jesus spoke these words during the final week of his human pilgrimage on earth – just prior to his death and resurrection. Jesus was in Bethany, one of his favourite places of retreat and rest. He was at a dinner given in his honour by those closest to him. It seems that perhaps others besides Jesus had a growing understanding of what was soon to happen. During the meal Mary anointed Jesus' feet with a bottle of expensive perfume and then wiped his feet with her hair. It is not difficult to imagine the deeply meaningful atmosphere that such devotion would have produced among those gathered to share this meal together. This was a special occasion in a location where Jesus would have felt at home, among people he loved.

In such an atmosphere, the words of Judas rang hollow. 'Why wasn't this perfume sold and the money given to the poor?'[16] Jesus, patient as ever, simply replied by explaining that on this occasion the perfume was for a different purpose – to anoint him for his burial. For although the poor would always be there, he wouldn't be. As Brian McLaren points out, to use these words to justify ignoring the plight of the poor doesn't make sense when you consider the original context or, indeed, when you consider the clear commands of the rest of Scripture concerning the poor. Here Jesus is quoting from Deuteronomy 15, which says that the poor will always be around. The text goes on to say, 'Therefore I command you to be open-handed towards your brothers and towards the poor and needy in your land.'[17] As McLaren reminds us, 'It's risky business to superficially quote Jesus!'[18]

Jim Wallis points out that in Mark's version the incident actually takes place in the home of Simon the Leper[19] – again highlighting Jesus' concern for the poor, which he is passing on to his disciples. Wallis extrapolates what Jesus is trying to convey to his disciples: 'You know who we spend time with, who we share meals with, who listens to our message, who we focus our attention on. You've been watching me, and you know what my priorities are. You know who comes first in the Kingdom of God. So, you will always be near the poor, you'll always be with them, and you will always have the opportunity to share with them.'[20]

In fact, as the story in John unfolds it becomes increasingly uncomfortable for those who want to use this passage as a justification for doing nothing. John makes it clear that Judas said what he did not because he cared for the poor, but because the sale of that perfume would have meant more money in the common purse from which he helped himself. But where did this idea of selling the perfume come from? Was it just a bright idea he had on the spot? Did he think, 'If we'd sold that perfume I could have had the money myself'? I don't think so. If we read on in John's Gospel we find that, when Judas left in the middle of the last meal that Jesus shared with his disciples, the disciples didn't understand what was happening. In fact, John records that they thought he was leaving the room either to buy what was needed for the feast or to give something to the poor.[21]

It seems, therefore, that Jesus and his disciples had a common purse out of which they purchased provisions as they travelled. Out of that common purse they also provided for the needs of others as they came across them and sometimes, it seems, when given a gift in kind they sold it and either put the income in their common purse or gave the money to someone in need. The picture we have of Jesus and his disciples is of a group of people living very much hand to mouth as they travelled the length and breadth of Palestine. And yet they were constantly concerned with the plight of others and provided for them as they could. It was a lifestyle of concern for, and engagement with, the poor. In the light of that, we then see Jesus' words in a completely different light. Jesus is not saying, 'Forget the poor, they will always be there.' Rather, he is saying, 'The poor are important and we must embrace and help them in every way we can. But on this particular occasion, as I am preparing to die, it's OK to use this perfume for a different purpose.' Far from providing an exit clause for engagement with the poor, Jesus' words in John 12 actually challenge us to a lifestyle of involvement.[22]

3

Community

'We see those cigarette advertisements with the rugged cowboy riding around alone on a horse, and we think that is strength, when, really, it is like setting your soul down on a couch and not exercising it. The soul needs to interact with other people to be healthy.'

– *Donald Miller*[1]

One morning, just before eight o'clock, Shiny, Rachel and I were walking along the main seafront road in Bandra when we spotted a woman squatting at the side of the road. We had just spent half an hour with a group of people suffering from leprosy, drinking tea and chatting about how life was for them. This woman was on the other side of the road and looked to be huddled up in a bundle. There was something about her pose that indicated not all was right. We crossed the road, and as we got closer

> If all people are made in the image of God, all people need relationship to be fully human – just as God is in relationship as Father, Son and holy Spirit. The poor need community like everyone does. A key dimension to poverty is ostracism and marginalization. A key part of our work is to build supportive relationships and foster community.

we could tell that indeed she was in pain, but it was only when we were right next to her that we realized the reason why – she was having a baby! My horror quickly turned to relief that Rachel was there. Although Rachel was not a midwife, she'd had some basic midwifery lessons during her general nursing training. Rachel assessed the situation and decided that we'd need both a razor and a pair of clamps as well as a towel and some gloves. I offered to go and get them and, as the baby's head was already visible, I ran as fast as I could to the nearest hospital. Like all hospitals, they were used to people coming in to have babies – but not to men running in and asking for clamps and razors. But I persisted, and eventually I managed to speak with someone senior who allowed me to sign for them and back I ran. When I arrived, after what must have been a long twenty minutes for Rachel and Shiny, the little boy had already been born. Rachel was holding him in her arms, doing everything that she remembered from her training, and praying furiously. We clamped the cord, cut it and persuaded a sympathetic rickshaw driver to take us over to the hospital on the understanding that we would clean the rickshaw. Both mother and baby survived. Afterwards Rachel told me that she was grateful I'd been there as, being the father of three, she assumed I would have some idea what to do. How wrong she was!

When Claire, our oldest, was born at Landour Community Hospital at six and a half thousand feet in the Himalayan Mountains of North India, I held her in my arms within a few minutes of her birth. It was one of the most profound spiritual experiences of my life. I was awestruck by the amazing miracle of birth. In the days that followed I carried her around the school community where we were working, showing her off. People would look at me and then at Claire and say, 'Isn't she beautiful!' What they meant was, 'How did someone who looks like you manage to produce someone as beautiful as that?' But on a serious note, when each of our children was born the joy we experienced was profound because it was shared in community. People went out of their way to help and the meals they cooked, the clothes they washed and the jobs they covered for us were an expression of the love that is shared in community. Without it, our lives are barren.

What a contrast between the birth of my own child and the birth of this little boy at the side of the road. And it wasn't the fact that Claire was born in the somewhat sanitized security of a hospital ward. To me, the most profound contrast was the fact that Joan, my wife, gave birth within the context of a loving, supportive community whereas this woman was completely alone. Nobody else knew she was having a baby, nobody except us came to visit her in the hospital after the birth, nobody knew she was there. She lived her life on her own. She didn't have a community. She was alienated with no one to relate to. Giving birth to a child alone symbolizes, for me, what poverty is all about – isolation, alienation, marginalization. As Henri Nouwen wrote, 'Probably no word better summarizes the suffering of our times than the word "homeless." It reveals one of our deepest and most painful conditions, the condition of not having a sense of belonging, of not having a place where we can feel safe, cared for, protected, and loved.'[2]

But I encountered another striking contrast that day the little boy was born at the side of the road. For centuries, people with leprosy have suffered extraordinary exclusion from societies all over the world. At the time it was estimated there were seventy thousand lepers living in Mumbai, and most of them made their living by begging. Economically they were poor. The lepers with

whom Rachel, Shiny and I had spent time just before we
encountered the woman giving birth didn't own cars,
gadgets or mod-cons. But despite their marginalization
they had one thing of real significance: they had each
other, they had relationship, they had community. As we
sat with them and enjoyed a cup of tea we didn't hear
stories of pain, though there was much pain in their
lives. We heard stories of hope for the day ahead. We
laughed together. They were rich in relationship. They
shared what it was like to be dependent on the generosity of people to give their small change as they
graciously held out a tin to those who waited in their
cars for the traffic lights to turn green. Even their marginalization as a group by others in society could not
diminish the strength of relationship within their community. Just a little way down the road, a woman was
giving birth on her own.

Our Need for Relationship

Through our work among the poor, and particularly
among the destitute poor, we learned that one of
people's greatest needs is for relationship. I discovered
that when I met Rajesh.[3] That day as I was walking, at a
reasonably fast pace, to meet some people who were in
town, Rajesh stopped me in my tracks. I knew he wanted something, but in an effort to pass him off I suggested he give me a call and left him with my phone
number. I didn't expect to hear from him again. I did
hear, though, and then he came to visit. He came almost
weekly to tell me about his life and how things were
going. We would chat and sometimes pray and then he
would go back to the streets again. He had no home and
no community. I began to understand that the greatest

gift I could give him was my time, my undivided attention, my 'self'. Matthew Frost has made a similar observation from his own experiences.

> People often ask me what they can do either to help those living in poverty, or to serve God with increased passion. And the answer I give has nothing to do with money. It is: time. Make time. Unhurried time to get to know your neighbours, to appreciate the need on your doorstep, to volunteer practically. Poverty is not just an economic catastrophe; it isolates, it disempowers, it marginalizes. And the remarkable thing is this: when we allow poverty to come up close and personal it transforms us.[4]

One of the issues Western tourists often struggle with when they visit a city in the global south is what to do about those who beg. It can be disconcerting to have someone tug at your shirt or knock on your taxi window in such a persistent manner. People often struggle with whether or not they should give because they've heard that those who beg are controlled by someone else and therefore won't keep what they are given. They are also concerned lest the money they give will be squandered on drugs or alcohol instead of being used for something more nourishing. The vast majority of those who beg, however, will never turn away from conversation. If you begin chatting with a person who is begging, you very often discover they will forget that they were begging because now they are being treated like a human being. A transformation begins to occur when we treat people not like beggars but as people made in the image of God. Whether you give to a person begging or not is not really important. That you treat them as a real person, made in God's image just like you, is very important.

I remember one evening sitting in our flat in Mumbai and watching a TV programme that highlighted the plight of a family who lived in one of Glasgow's high-rise apartment blocks. The family had food on the table, clothes to wear, and a TV to watch. The children went to school. Economically they were in reasonable shape, yet they spoke of their despondency, the ostracism they felt, their lack of hope. They might have had just enough income to live without worry, but they had few relationships and little that gave meaning or purpose to their lives. While watching that programme from our flat in the heart of Mumbai I couldn't help but contrast the experience of that family with those we knew in Mumbai. We knew families who wouldn't eat that day unless they earned the money to feed their children; families who couldn't afford for their children not to work alongside them as they scoured the city streets for rubbish; families in which parents held down three or four jobs just to make enough money to send their children to school. The difference between the family in Scotland and these families we knew was that, despite the depth of their (economic) poverty, they had relationships that were strong; they had people who would miss them if they didn't come home at the end of the day; they had bonds of community that gave their lives meaning.

In the West, lack of community is one of the most crippling aspects of modern-day poverty. This kind of poverty is not 'in your face' as much as economic poverty is. We see economic poverty in children scrounging for food in rubbish dumps; in enlarged stomachs that visually signify malnutrition; in small children who don't have the energy to smile. But poverty of relationships, though not visible, is just as crippling – because it is poverty of the soul. When you take away relationship, you take away the essence of being human. Mother

Teresa instantly saw this on her visits to the West, and she mentioned it on more than one occasion.

> You, in the West, have millions of people who suffer such terrible loneliness and emptiness. They feel unloved and unwanted. These people are not hungry in the physical sense, but they are in another way. They know they need something more than money, yet they don't know what it is.[5]

The Image of God as Community

In Genesis 1 there is an interesting shift that takes place in verse 26 as the creation of humankind is introduced. God has just brought the light, the waters, the land, the animals and more into being through his command. But as humankind is created God says, 'Let us make human beings in our image, in our likeness, and let them rule over the fish of the sea and the birds of the air, over the livestock, over all the earth, and over all the creatures that move along the ground.'[6] This shift is an expression of God as community – the Father, Son and Spirit all engaged in the creation story. As John Calvin wrote,

> Hitherto God has been introduced simply as commanding; now, when he approaches the most excellent of all his works, he enters into consultation. God certainly might have commanded by his bare word what he wished to be done; but he chose to give this tribute to the excellency of man, that he would, in a manner, enter into consultation concerning his creation.[7]

This is not the place for a discourse on the Trinity, one of the truths that even the most gifted theologian struggles to communicate effectively. However, at its most basic level we understand that God was not alone. Within God there was communion and fellowship – community. Such understanding is enhanced as Jesus himself makes reference both to his relationship with the Father and to his oneness with him.

> The world must learn that I love the Father and that I do exactly what my Father has commanded me.[8]

> All things have been committed to me by my Father. No-one knows the Son except the Father, and no-one knows the Father except the Son and those to whom the Son chooses to reveal him.[9]

> I and the Father are one.[10]

There is, in the relationship between the Father, Son and Spirit, complete trust, unity and love. This intimacy was not developed or grown but was inherent in the very existence of God. To be made in God's image is to be made with the capacity and longing for relationship such as this. Indeed, God said right at the point of creation, 'It is not good for the man to be alone.'[11] Doug Baker suggests that it was not possible for Adam to 'image' God without a covenant partner because the relationship they had was a covenantal one. His main thesis is that the 'image of God' is not so much about inherent characteristics but about our purpose and role, and he suggests that the future (eschatological) outcome of being made in God's image is the kind of oneness Jesus speaks about in John 17. Bryant Myers makes the point that, fundamentally, a person is only fully human when they are in relationship with both God and other people – which is an outworking of being made in the image of a Trinitarian God.[13] There is no doubt, then, that relationship is a key aspect of how God's image is reflected in humankind. As Chris Wright says, 'relationship is part of the very being of God, and therefore also part of the very being of humanity, created in his image'.[14]

When I was visiting the Oasis team in Johannesburg recently I had the chance to visit the Apartheid Museum there. It was so different from my childhood visits to museums in the UK. It was very experiential, as I was bombarded by the noise and visuals of injustice. Part of the experience is to sit in a cell similar to the one in which Nelson Mandela spent so much time in solitary confinement. It had never really dawned on me before why solitary confinement was such a horrendous punishment. But as I sat on the floor of that cell for just a few minutes I realized that the nature of this punishment hits right at the heart of personhood. It can break people, even destroy them, because God made us for relationship. And when all relationships are taken away from us, when we can no longer see other people, speak to other people or respond to other people, we in some way cease to be human. Our need for community stems from the very fabric of our being as image-bearers of God – Father, Son, and Holy Spirit.

Poverty as Marginalization and Exclusion

When we understand the centrality of relationship to what it means to be human, we can begin to appreciate why poverty is most clearly seen in marginalization and exclusion. Marginalization and exclusion occur when relationships break down and do not reflect God's original purpose. This is a result of the fall. It is not long

In His Image

after sin enters the scene in Genesis 3 that exclusion begins and, as the biblical record unfolds, it becomes an accepted part of life. We first see its consequences in Cain and Abel, but as we progress through the Old Testament we find exclusion written on almost every page. People exclude one another on the basis of gender, age, nationality, belief, colour and so many other characteristics. It is the ultimate punishment that lies in the hands of all people. If there is someone I want to punish, I ignore them and don't allow them into my world, my community.

What is tragic today is that in the church we so often model what the rest of the world is doing. Society excludes people on the basis of all the distinctions mentioned above and a few more besides. Sadly, the church often does the same. Sometimes the only difference is that in the church we create even stricter barriers in order to 'preserve our own righteousness'. I will never forget what I witnessed at the wedding of one of our staff members who was part of the initial team that set up work in the red-light area of Mumbai. A whole group of girls from the brothels had been invited for the celebration and joined in the festivities. As they did, the unease of some of the other guests was palpable – what were a bunch of prostitutes doing at a middle-class wedding?

But I have also witnessed such wonderful inclusion and acceptance in the church, most notably modelled by 'Valley of Praise', the church we were part of during our years in Mumbai. Ivan Raskino, who started the church and was its senior pastor, is one of those people who models love and acceptance to all – irrespective of where they have come from, what they have done, or who they have become. In fact, the church started as a place of safety and community for those who were most broken. Ivan would walk the streets at night, pick up those who were drunk, pray for them and then gently lay them back down on the pavement. In the early years of the church, because it was full of drug addicts, girls from the brothels and those who lived on the streets, Ivan recalls that he never knew what to expect at services. An occasional fight even broke out. Slowly but surely, this group of broken people found God's acceptance through the acceptance that Ivan and Melanie (his wife) and others extended to them. It was a privilege to be a part of that. When I think of a God-centred, inclusive, real community I think of 'Valley of Praise'. The words of Samuel Escobar echo the experiences of so many in that church.

> Life in the warmth of the Christian community brings with it an awareness of belonging, in place of alienation; of family life, in place of an orphan life; of hospitality in place of hostility; of feeling oneself to be somebody, in place of being a nobody.[15]

These are some of the marks of the type of community we must seek to build. In this community people are accepted for who they are and are able to be real. In this community each individual is valued as an image bearer of God and not judged on outward appearance or on the specific contribution he or she is able to make. We must build communities where relationships are supportive, where celebration happens often, and where people can journey in life and faith seeking truth for themselves rather than simply accepting prescribed dogma. Such communities are messy but real.

Jesus Modelled an Inclusive Community

Jesus called people to be part of a community that travelled with him around Palestine. This group included
both the ordinary and the excluded, and everyone had
the privilege not just of learning through his teaching
but also of learning through being with him. It was, as
John later records, not so much what Jesus said but who
he was that had this profound impact on them. They
came to taste, see and understand him as both Messiah
and Son of God.[16] As Rob Bell points out, the point of
being the disciple of a rabbi was not to gather knowledge
in order to regurgitate it but to become like your rabbi,
doing what the rabbi would do. Rabbis would select
their own disciples from the best of the best, but 'Jesus
took some boys who didn't make the cut and changed
the course of human history.'[17] And the community they
became, with Jesus at the centre, included all the things
you would expect: squabbling over who was the best;
falling asleep at the point of their master's greatest need;
questioning the motives of the disciples of other rabbis.
One of the disciples even turned traitor and another
wouldn't admit he had had any association with Jesus at
all. This was an ordinary bunch of people Jesus brought
into this inclusive community to live with him.

In John 4 Jesus is in a place he is not supposed to be,
talking with a person he is not supposed to talk to, saying something he is not supposed to say. Real rabbis
wouldn't pass through Samaria because the Samaritans
were half-breeds – half-Jewish, half-Assyrian. The Jews
despised the Samaritans. Real rabbis would take a much
longer route around Samaria in order to avoid the kind
of encounter that Jesus appears to relish. Because it was
the middle of the day, the woman shouldn't really have
been at the well either. Perhaps she was there at the

hottest hour of the day because she didn't want to meet the other women, who would usually draw water at dusk or dawn – we don't know. As a Jew, a man and a rabbi Jesus should have avoided this woman. But he didn't. He willingly entered into conversation with her – no wonder the disciples were surprised when they caught up with him. Jesus modelled an inclusive approach to all within a culture where it was black and white whom he was expected to include – and to exclude.

Jesus did it again when he entered Jericho one day and struck up a conversation with Zacchaeus. And then he actually invited himself to Zacchaeus' house, which got the locals talking. Why? Because everyone knew there were certain kinds of people you should avoid, including tax collectors, but Jesus appeared to seek them out deliberately. Not only did Jesus seek them out, but he also shared meals with them. In most cultures even today, sharing a meal is a symbol of community. Jesus was doing more than accepting dinner invitations. He was joining in community with these people. What really upset the religious leaders of his day was that Jesus related to the Samaritan woman, Zacchaeus and many others as human beings. He gave time to building relationships with people the religious leaders deemed unworthy of relationship. Jesus reached out to people the religious leaders thought should be left alone and he treated them with respect and preserved their dignity.

Mark 5 records an incident within an incident. While Jesus was on his way to the home of Jairus, who was a synagogue ruler, someone who wished to remain anonymous touched Jesus with the hope of getting better. This woman was opposite to Jairus in many different respects. He was a man, she was a woman; he was wealthy, she was poor; he appealed to Jesus on someone else's behalf, she sought help on her own behalf; he came to Jesus up front and publicly, she stole up from behind; he verbalized his request, she was silent. The contrasts between the two couldn't be starker. But the main difference between the two, of course, was that Jairus was a respected member of the community and this woman had been ostracized. The bleeding she'd suffered for 12 years would have meant that she was permanently unclean and unable to join in worship or community life. She acted as she did, silently coming to Jesus from behind, because that was the role assigned to her by society – the role of someone who has been excluded. Jairus, on the other hand, had no problem voicing his request. After all, he was part of the included elite. But then a strange thing happened. After the woman was healed, simply by touching Jesus' robe, Jesus wanted to know who had touched him. He wanted her to go public with what had happened. We don't know for certain why, but perhaps Jesus wanted all who were there to know that this woman, who had been pushed to the edges of society, could once again be brought back into community life. It was now acceptable to invite her round for a meal! That seems the most likely reason why Jesus asked, 'Who touched my clothes?'[18] Salvation for this woman was not simply about believing in Jesus as the healer, which no doubt she did from that day on, but it was also about her being restored to wholeness within her community. That was what Jesus said to her as he pronounced the blessing, 'Go in peace'. Although this is the way it is often translated, '*shalom*' actually means much more than 'peace'. It expresses the concept of fullness of life in every area. As Rob Bell says of this incident,

> When Jesus tells the woman to go in peace, he is placing the blessing of God on all of her. Not just her physical body. He

is blessing her with God's presence on her entire being. And this is because for Jesus, salvation is holistic in nature. For Jesus, being saved or reconciled to God involves far more than just the saving of your physical body or your soul – it involves all of you.[19]

The way that Jesus related to those who were ostracized in the context of his day stood out in stark contrast to the behaviour of other religious leaders. The expectation was that religious leaders would understand and abide by the strict rules that kept people apart, and Jesus' failure to maintain this separation both surprised and angered those in authority. If they could come up with a reason to keep people separated, then the religious leaders of Jesus' day would do so. To all intents and purposes it was apartheid. Jesus showed scant regard for such rules and regulations. He often touched people or allowed them to touch him.

In many parts of the world, the worst impact that HIV infection can have is to ostracize people from others in their community. Things are somewhat better now than they were ten years ago – at least in some parts of the world – but still, like leprosy before it, this disease has caused ostracism on a massive scale. That was a key reason why Oasis set up a centre a couple of hours' drive from Mumbai where women who were marginalized in their own communities due to their HIV status could find a place of hope – a community. Through a series of miracles beginning with the recruitment of Kevin Potter, who directed this project, God opened the way for this centre to become a reality.

Often women discover that they are HIV positive through blood tests that are required because of a pregnancy or some other medical condition. When a woman discovers this first, the assumption is that she was the one to first be infected, and often she is blamed for infecting her husband – when the opposite is usually the case. We found that it was most often the husband who picked up the infection while visiting the red-light area (where statistics place the infection rate at 60 – 70%), and his wife would be an innocent party infected through her husband. While the husband lived, his wife would care for him. When he died, she might be discarded and any property they owned would be taken by his family. When Joan and I took Shobha up to the centre one wet monsoon day, she brought all she possessed in a couple of plastic bags – a plate, a cup and a few clothes. Since her infection had been discovered she had been forced to eat in a corner on her own, using her own cutlery. The centre, located a few hours' drive from Mumbai, was the only place where women and their children could find respite together. It became Shobha's community.

Relationship at the Heart of any Programme

In many ways, the projects and programmes Oasis set up were really only vehicles for creating relationships among those we served. For it is only ever through relationship that transformation begins to take place. Programmes that train, educate, heal or advocate can help make a difference in people's lives, but if the programmes end up being about statistics and targets and success, as is often the temptation, then little transformation will take place. Projects and programmes on their own never bring transformation. Only people do that. Bryant Myers reminds us that

> Transformation is about transforming relationships, and relationships are transformed by people. Techniques and

programs only fulfil their promise when holistic practitioners use them with the right attitude, the right mindset, and
professionalism.[20]

I have recently come across an organization in the UK
called 'The Relationship Foundation' which, among other
things, is seeking to demonstrate the clear connection that
exists between relationships and well-being. It is clear
from all the statistics that increased wealth does not bring
increased well-being, yet many decisions at a political level
seem to be made on the basis of increasing GDP which,
when analysed, can be seen to have a detrimental impact
on relationships and community cohesion. I have no doubt
that relationships have to be the core of well-being because
we're made in the image of a relational God. Poverty is at
its worst when people don't have others with whom they
can relate. A key aspect of our work among the poor is to
foster relationship and community. Michael Schluter, who
together with David Lee wrote the *The R Factor*, makes the
point that very often government economic policies in the
UK do not help to fos-
ter healthy relationships
because they tend to deal
with both the levels and the
distribution of wealth. They
may help to increase GDP,
but a biblical understanding of real quality of life
encompasses a much wider
sphere of concerns, including 'the quality of social,
political, and economic relationships'. He calls this
'relational well-being'.[21]

> If all people are made in the image of God, all people need relationship to be fully human – just as God is in relationship as Father, Son and Holy Spirit. The poor need community like everyone does. A key dimension to poverty is ostracism and marginalization. A key part of our work is to build supportive relationships and foster community.

4

Wholeness

Because of our multidimensional nature, mission cannot be anything less than an integrated and integral enterprise.
— *Jean-Paul Heldt*[1]

If you visit most of the mega-cities in the world today, and many smaller ones too, you will experience the growing phenomenon of children who live their lives on the streets of those cities. Statistics have suggested that there are, at a minimum, over 100 million[2] of these children in the world's cities today. The term 'street children' is dubious and often misunderstood because it refers to several categories of children who spend a significant portion of their time out in the open and not where a sane society would want them – in a place of love and security. Many of those who are called street children do have a place that they return to at night where they sleep – though if your

Because all people are made in the image of God, every aspect of a person's life is important to God. God has also created us as whole people, such that every part of a person's life is integrated with other parts. We must therefore treat the poor not as bodies to be fed or as souls to be won but as whole people for whom God desires fullness of life.

definition of a 'home' is more than a roof over your head at night then the vast majority of these children are, in fact, 'homeless'. It is a wonder that, in the twenty-first century, we accept this situation as normal. There is something chillingly wrong with a world society that allows many of its weakest members to suffer such alienation. While alienation would be bad enough, the situation is in fact much worse than that. Many individuals and governments consider street children to be a problem. Not only do they assume that the children are responsible for their own predicament, but they also often assume they are criminals who would steal at any opportunity. Some governments round these children up like cattle and ship them off to detention centres – not because the children might benefit from this in some way, but rather because some dignitary is coming to town and visitors who see street children will not go away with a good impression of the city.[3] These children suffer persecution and alienation as well as the physical rigours of life on the streets. But, in addition to all of that, each one of these precious children carries a different story of pain. Scars are deeply etched in their psyches from the traumas they have faced – traumas that, in many cases, drove them to the streets in the first place.

Those who work amongst street children, however, will tell you that even though they have been alienated, scarred and traumatized – and regardless of the pain of the experiences they have faced – every single one of them has a great capacity for love, loyalty, compassion and mercy. Each one of them has been made in the image of God and that image, though sometimes hidden, is always there and often visible.

Vittel lived for many years in one of the busiest train stations in Mumbai. For a couple of years he came to one of our programmes during the day to learn a skill and returned to his home on the streets each night. One day he called Dave, the project leader, and told him there was a girl, Shahanaz, who needed help. Vittel had met her at the station and discovered that she had just arrived in the city. She'd escaped from a traumatic home situation and hoped to begin life afresh. (The vast majority of children who leave home because of abuse or trauma go to the cities in the hope that life in the bright lights will bring a turn in their fortunes. The reality is that, in most cases, it gets worse.) Shahanaz was at her most vulnerable, but her meeting with Vittel literally saved her life. He knew that within a matter of days the pimps would swoop and offer her some nice job that would never materialize and instead they would sell her into the brothels. And when Vittel phoned Dave to tell him about Shahanaz, the image of God was evident in his life because love, mercy and compassion are a reflection of God's character. These qualities are seen in street children more often than most of us might think.

When we began working in Mumbai in the early 1990s I knew that one of the groups we would be working among were street children, but I had no experience of what that would mean. Early on, though, I was introduced to two women who had registered a small organization as a means of helping street children. I was privileged to be involved in their work at Kandivili station in the northern suburbs of city. I was struck at once by Juliette and Charmaine's gifts and compassion for the kids they sought to help. One day the three of us were walking down the steps on to the station when we saw a boy who was walking slowly while holding on to the rail. It was obvious he was in pain, so we stopped to find out what was going on. He explained that pain in his back prevented him from walking with any freedom, and it had become steadily worse over recent weeks. His name was Chottu. We decided he needed proper medical assistance and so we arranged for his admission into one of the hospitals we knew would give him good care. They soon discovered that the problem originated not in his back but in his lungs. Unfortunately, the TB was so advanced that it had impacted his spine – hence his pain and difficulty in walking. They made Chottu a brace, which he hated to wear, and after three weeks decided that he was far enough along the road to recovery to be discharged. All he needed to do, the doctor said, was to keep on taking his medication. So we paid the bill but didn't know exactly what to do next. He couldn't go back to the streets in the condition he was in, and the other possible places he might stay didn't materialize, so he came to live with us. That meant that Joan, my wife, could ensure he took his medication and wore his brace.

Chottu was probably about twelve at the time, though he couldn't remember his exact age and no one else knew. He had ended up on the streets when his father died back in his village and his mother brought him to the city. He didn't know exactly what happened next, just that he was on his own and needed to survive. This had happened several years before we met him. Like so many others in his situation, Chottu used all the initiative and inner resources that God had given him to survive – and survive he had. He did small jobs for people to earn a few rupees and found favour with people who helped him and gave him food. Like many others, he had just made a go of life. He lived for each day and was unaware and unconcerned about what the future might hold. He didn't stay with us for long as the wisdom of the doctor was that his extensive TB meant it was too risky for him to live in a small flat with our three small children.[4] He went to live with John and Chris, two other staff members, who cared for him for several months before we were able to find a more permanent home where he and three others could live.

A few months later Chottu was back in the hospital and it didn't look good. Chickenpox had turned into pneumonia and his body, weak from the TB medication, was battling to survive. After a few days spent in the hospital, often in a state of delirium, his brief life ended. As I stood by his graveside I realized that each one of the approximately ten people who had come to his burial had only known him for a few short months. And we all wondered whether there was anything else we could have done. We had such mixed emotions as we pondered what seemed such a waste. This young boy had been so gifted, so talented, so loving and generous. He was also a boy of faith. Not only would he welcome our prayers for him, but he would also volunteer to pray for others in need around him. Why had his life ended before it had really begun? At the same time we also knew that now, after years of difficulty and pain, he was at last free from suffering. He was in a place where all tears are wiped away, where there is no more crying or death or mourning, or pain.

Back at Kandivili station we ended up focusing on the older group of kids, those over fourteen years old. We met up with them at the station several times each week, taught them about God, and tried to help them deal with issues they were facing. It wasn't working. Meeting up a couple of times a week didn't seem to be making much difference in their lives. So, even though it was an hour's journey away, we decided that we would bring them to our flat to meet with them there. We did that for several months, but that wasn't working either. It seemed that we would never have an impact on their lives by being with them just part of the time. We needed to be with them the whole day to model what it was like to live a life with God at the heart. That led us to the idea of setting up a small business that would train and employ these young people. This would enable us to model life rather than simply teach about God. I was put in touch with Paul Das. Paul was involved in many things, one of which was a papier-mâché initiative he had set up in Bangalore to provide training and employment to disadvantaged young people. It seemed the ideal skill, and Paul generously let us learn the technology and helped us enormously in setting up something similar in Mumbai.

One of the first boys to join the project was a young man called Rajesh. He was brought along by some other boys who all lived at Dadar railway station. The railway station had been his home since he was eight years old, and trouble had been his constant companion. It had all started back home in Andhra Pradesh when his father died and his mother remarried. For some reason his relationship with his stepfather was constantly fraught, and one day Rajesh decided he'd had enough and he left. Soon after arriving in Mumbai he was absorbed into a peer group that collected empty plastic water bottles and either sold them for scrap or refilled them and sold them at a highly discounted price. Once he had enough money, Rajesh rented a space on top of a station tea-stall where he could sleep, dry his clothes and keep the few possessions he had. For eight hours a day that space was his. If he overslept he didn't need an alarm clock because the next tenant would wake him up for his eight-hour stint.

Like most street children who have been badly let down over and over again for many years, Rajesh could not trust anyone. Even when he was treated fairly and paid well for work he'd done, his initial response was always to question the amount. He didn't know what a trusting relationship was like. And it's impossible to develop a sense of self-worth without significant trusting relationships. When trust is developed mutually people can begin to understand their value – without trust, people see themselves as valueless. That is why, in the early weeks, Rajesh constantly talked about himself as a 'no gooder'. He repeated that phrase throughout the day.

Rajesh didn't just need a job or money or a place to sleep. He needed relationship; he needed friendship; he needed help with his health; he needed an advocate; he needed a family; he needed to be treated as a human being. Dave, who led the project, became not just his employer but also his counsellor, his father and mother and brother, his nurse, his teacher. Dave and the other staff modelled what it meant to be human, to be alive, to know God. Rajesh didn't just get a glimpse of that – he felt and tasted it.

Over the months and years Rajesh's skills grew and, slowly but surely, he began to trust others. Although he was still living on the streets, he kept himself cleaner, his face brightened, he smiled and he learnt to pray. God was clearly working in his life.

We weren't able to have an impact on Rajesh and Chottu and many others like them because we had specialist knowledge or skills. Nor was it because we ran a good business or because we were good at explaining what God was like. I believe we saw God at work in their lives because we learnt early on that when we view those who are marginalized and rejected by society as whole people and work with them in an integrated way, we can bring the gospel in all its fullness – the gospel that is for the whole of a person's life.

Holism in Context

The word 'holism' entered the vocabulary of the evangelical church in the Western world as it re-awoke to its responsibility for a wider mandate than evangelism.[5] Holism came to be defined as the combination of preaching the gospel and social engagement; of word and deed; of concern for people's physical and spiritual lives. As the charismatic movement grew in strength and presence a third dimension was sometimes added to holism – that of miracle, power or wonder.[6] Since all of this began to take root during the 1950s, 1960s and 1970s, a variety of people have added to the thinking in this area. And yet, for many, word and deed continue to sit in an uncomfortable alliance.

Not long ago I attended some meetings focused on the issues of street children. In the course of the discussions, one person made the following comment concerning the approach we should take: 'It is far more important that children have a future in heaven than food to eat today.'[7] This person has a heart for these kids and has given her life to work amongst them, but I think she reflected the unease that some people have as they try to balance preaching the gospel with social engagement. Her comment implied that God places a person's spiritual well-being above their physical or emotional well-being. Many books and articles have been written about this subject and it has been the topic of endless debate at conferences around the world. Chris Wright, in his wonderful in-depth tome on mission, suggests that speaking about the primacy of evangelism can create some 'uncomfortable consequences' – even though he has a lot of sympathy with that position.[8] David Bosch, in his great work *Transforming Mission*, gives a helpful overview of how the thinking in this area has developed.

While he acknowledges that 'The relationship between the evangelistic and societal dimensions of the Christian mission constitutes one of the thorniest areas in theology and practice of mission,'[9] he also reminds us that

> Missionary literature, but also missionary practice, emphasizes that we should find a way beyond every schizophrenic position and minister to people in their total need, that we should involve individuals as well as society, soul and body, present and future, in our ministry of salvation.[10]

What is encouraging today is the increasing move towards a more integrated understanding of how we engage with people. Malcolm Duncan, who until recently led the 'Faithworks' movement that seeks to mobilize local congregations to effectively engage with their communities, says that

> Integral mission tries to move away from the language of evangelism at one end of the spectrum and social action on the other, to a holistic and joined up approach which inseparably links actions and words in the lives of both individual Christians and local churches.[11]

Many others echo this thinking in their writings. Bryant Myers makes the point that this dichotomy is the result of modernity, which separated the physical and spiritual realms of life. He says that this is what has caused Christians to believe that God's redemptive work only takes place in the spiritual realm, leaving the rest of life 'seemingly, to the devil'.[12] Since all of life is God's domain, we need to be concerned with people in a holistic and integrated way.

A leader with Oasis in South Africa recently told me that he went into a Christian bookshop and asked if they had any good books on engaging with people who have HIV/AIDS. He was shocked to be told, rather abruptly, 'This is a Christian bookstore – I suggest you go to the secular bookshop on the second floor if you want a book on that subject!' Christians in general have yet to grasp that all of life is God's domain and God's concern. Books on AIDS should stand next to books on prayer in any bookshop that calls itself Christian.

In the community where I live in the UK, and indeed in many such communities around the country, great numbers of people are suffering as the result of being trapped in a cycle of debt. Some find themselves in this position because they lived beyond their means for a time on available credit provided by the banks. But others are suffering now because their employment or family circumstances changed and they ended up with commitments they could not fulfil. Still others are victims of the benefit system itself. Someone in our church community had the vision to set up a centre to provide advice and counsel to those in such situations. In five years, over seven hundred people have received assistance. Aspects of people's lives have been redeemed, and people have seen God's presence in more tangible ways than would otherwise have been the case. The fact that a local church is running a programme like this shows that they understand God's concern for the whole of a person's life – not just the spiritual part. I hope that our local Christian bookshop has some books on debt – I haven't checked to see!

Holism Motivated by the Integrated Nature of Personhood

We should be involved in people's lives in a holistic and integrated way because all of life is God's domain. But there is another key reason. Instead of starting from the place of our responsibility, let's start with the recipient of mission – the person or people to whom we are relating. Each person has been made in the image of God and, as we have said, God's image is present in people in their totality – body and soul. As G.C. Berkouwer says, 'Scripture's emphasis on the whole man as the image of God has triumphed time and time again over all objections and opposing principles.'[13] However, we should view people as whole people not only because the whole person reflects God's image, but also because in God's design there is an integration of life's different components that cannot be separated from one another. We have been created so that mind, body, and soul work as an integrated unity.

Sometimes when we look at this issue in Oasis I will ask one of our staff members to tell us as a group about her life. She will talk about her job, her home, her friends, her health, her church, and other aspects of her life. With a little prompting we can usually glean some information about the person's financial position, relationship to God and a range of other concerns that make up that person's life. Then there is one key question we ask that person: What is the relationship between the different components of your life? In other words, does your financial position have any impact on your sense of well-being? Do issues at work affect your spiritual well-being? If you don't have enough money, does that impact your health? The answer, of course, is always 'Yes.' Not having enough money might well affect my health, and if relationships at work are not good then that will probably have consequences in terms of my relationship with God too. This is because God has made us to be integrated beings. Try as you might, it is literally impossible to live a 'compartmentalized' life. To some extent and at certain times, we all focus on particular things in our lives to escape the pain of some other area. When I've had an argument with my wife, for example, I might go and do some exercise or invest my energies in my work, but the truth remains that we do those things to try to escape the pain of being integrated. None of us like it when our spouse comes home from a bad day at work and starts an argument about something petty – but the fact that they do that is actually a good sign. It's a healthy indication that he or she is integrated. Issues in one part of life always impact the rest of who we are.

After talking with an Oasis group about this concept of integration, sometimes we then go on to ask the following question: Which area is the most important part of your life to you or to God? Is God more concerned for your health, employment, friendships or relationship with him? While people might have had ready answers to that question before our discussion about integration, when we ask this afterwards there is usually a pause as people think through the implications of being created as integrated beings. It becomes clear that to ask which is more important to God is the wrong question. God is concerned about every area of your life because, fundamentally, he is interested in you. God has an integrated concern for you and your complete wellbeing. When Jesus was with a large crowd of hungry people he didn't tell his disciples, 'Oh well, these poor people are all hungry, but it's OK because at least they've decided to follow me so they'll have a great time in heaven.' No! Jesus, we are told, had compassion on them and suggested to the disciples that they feed them. We often miss the humour in the Bible, but surely this must have been said with a bit of a wink and a nod and a wry smile. After all, where were the disciples going to find enough food to feed five thousand people?[14]

If we do want to answer the question regarding which aspect of a person's life is most important to God, the answer must come out of the context of that person's circumstances. At a given point in a person's life God may well be most concerned about their hunger, at another time about the pain of a relationship gone wrong, and at another about the fact they just lost their job. This is an amazing truth to grasp about God: he is concerned about you and me as integrated beings with multiple needs. God knows that many things affect our sense of well-being, joy and purpose – and he is concerned for them all.

Integration Reflects God's Image

The Bible understands humankind, made in God's image, as integrated beings. As Doug Baker and Anthony Hoekema both reiterate,

> Humanity as a whole and human beings considered as individuals are not seen in either the Hebrew Bible or the Christian Bible as spirits inhabiting bodies, or as intellects lashed to ethical concerns. Throughout the Bible, spirit, soul, body, mind, strength, imagination, and emotion are all interwoven to form one creature, the human.[15]

> We may summarize our discussion of the biblical words used to describe the various aspects of man as follows: man must be understood as a unitary being. He has a physical side and a mental or spiritual side, but we must not separate these two. . . . He or she must be seen in his or her totality, not as a composite of different 'parts'. This is the clear teaching of both Old and New Testaments.[16]

Integrated beings reflect God's image. Neither did God limit this concept of integration in creation to human beings. The principles of integration and interdependency are a key component of the whole created order. Our ecosystem, for example, is completely interdependent. When we interfere with one aspect, other parts suffer the repercussions. We are beginning to understand this more than we ever have through the present ecological crisis in which we find ourselves.

A holistic or integrated approach to the work we do, then, is not first and foremost a programmatic thing – it is not a combination of preaching the gospel and social action. Rather, it is an approach we take as individuals to the people among whom we work. Do we see those we serve as integrated beings made in the image of God with multiple needs for which God is concerned? Do we treat them as bodies to be fed or clothed? Souls to be saved? Minds to be educated? Or do we see them as whole people, reflecting the way they (and we) have been created? As Bryant Myers says, 'Holism is for the most part a state of mind or attitude.' When I think of Rajesh and Chottu, the reason I believe we had a significant impact on their lives is because we saw them as whole people and got involved in their lives as whole people.

We were once working in a slum where others were involved also. Another organization was conducting an AIDS awareness programme and trying to reach as many people as possible. The pastor of the church with whom we were working in partnership told me that one day he had come across someone who was suffering from AIDS. So he asked the organization doing the AIDS awareness if they could help that person. He was stunned by their reply. 'We can't,' they said. 'We only do awareness. We can't help someone who is suffering in that way.' This is remarkable but true.

Sometimes the constraints of funding detract us from our biblical mandate to be holistic. Some organizations offer grants that dictate the numbers of people the grant recipient needs to impact. There is nothing wrong with that in itself, but what can happen is that it becomes the determining factor of how or even whether we relate to people, and that is wrong. 'We don't have time to help you. All you are to us is another statistic to say we achieved our goal of educating (or immunizing, or whatever the service provided is).' That, in my humble opinion, is wrong – though it happens frequently.

Once we grasp this paradigm – the integrated nature of all people – then it isn't a huge leap to understand that our mission must embrace all aspects of life. People do not live in isolation. They live in relationship with others, with nature and with God. Each of these relationships will have an impact on their wellbeing, and therefore all of them are important in God's sight. In our engagement among those who are poor we must never forget that God is concerned with the totality of their lives – and not just with isolated aspects of their lives. Ray Bakke, who has been a pioneer in engagement among the urban poor in the United States, has reflected historically on how we lost this perspective that the church once understood.

Historians have told us that the personal lives and public laws of many Western countries were shaped by this holistic work of God. But for nearly a century now, the God of most evangelicals has been withdrawing on an extended retreat to the friendly confines of Christian hearts and minds. Those who preach that we should only save souls, preach, and plant churches without getting involved socially in society are really doing two things: one, admitting to the irrelevance of the gospel over large sectors of modern life and, secondly, tacitly supporting the socially sinful status quo. Neither fulfils the vision of transformed societies and model cities that we glimpse in Isaiah 58:65; Jeremiah 29; Ezekiel 16, and a host of other texts.[18]

At its heart, holism is about treating those we work amongst as integrated people made in the image of God. A holistic organization is not one that combines evangelism with social action but one in which staff all treat people as integrated beings. This is Jesus' approach – feeding the hungry, engaging in conversation, healing the sick, even turning water into wine. He didn't preach and see everything else as a distraction. He engaged in lots of things because he was holistic in his approach – and so we must be too.

This has implications for both our programmes and our structures, because these can either empower people to approach their work in this way or they can cripple them from doing so. Good organizational structures allow those working for that organization to have flexibility so that they can engage with people in this integrated way. When job descriptions are too rigid and goals too specialized and narrow, people who want to serve can become so confined that they have no time to treat people as people. And we end up with programmes that are not holistic. Organizational structure, programme objectives and the mindset of those who work with us all help to determine whether or not we take a holistic approach. There needs to be some creative thinking about how all three work together in the light of our beliefs concerning the nature of human life.

> Because all people are made in the image of God, every aspect of a person's life is important to God. God has also created us as whole people, such that every part of a person's life is integrated with other parts. We must therefore treat the poor not as bodies to be fed or as souls to be won but as whole people for whom God desires fullness of life.

5

Change

> God's terrible insistence on human freedom is so absolute that he granted us the power to live as though he did not exist, to spit in his face, to crucify him.
>
> – *Philip Yancey*[1]

Zarine grew up in a reasonably well-to-do Muslim family in Kolkatta in West Bengal. She had siblings to play with and food was plentiful, so there was little that troubled her in the early years. When she was about eight years old, though, her mother was poisoned by her father's second wife and Zarine was sent to live with one of her older sisters and her husband. Not long after, when she was just ten years old, her marriage was arranged. But when that didn't work out she was sent home and then went to live with another sister's family. Things were not going well. While Zarine was

> Because all people are made in the image of God, we respect that all people must make their own decisions about who they want to be. Each individual must plot his or her own path. We choose not to force our way on the poor, but rather we come to support, encourage, and cheer from the sidelines — knowing that change comes from within.

dancing at a festival, a woman approached her and offered her the chance to learn a trade and work as a handbag painter in the city. Zarine was happy to accept as it promised her a way out of her problems. What Zarine didn't know, of course, was that the woman was a trafficker who earned money by selling girls into prostitution. Zarine found herself in Mumbai, serving customers in a posh flat. When she at first refused she was given electric shock treatment, so she soon became compliant and after a few months was in a place where she simply accepted the nightly abuse as her lot. She was twelve years old.

It was six years later that some of our staff met Zarine while visiting the brothels. She had only recently discovered that she was HIV positive. At first, like all the girls there, she was cautious in speaking with our staff. But, over time, she warmed to the strangers who would visit with no specific agenda except to assist the girls in any way they could and to constantly remind them that God was on their side. By that time Zarine had worked long enough to have a fair amount of freedom, and so she could come and go more than most of the other girls. Leaving the brothels permanently, however, was not something she had considered in a while because for her, like so many others, going home wasn't an option. A few months after the initial contact she decided to accept an invitation to attend a retreat organized by one of the churches in the city. Miraculously, the brothel keeper gave her permission to go and it was there that God met her in a very special way. She began to pray and see God answer her prayers, but she continued to battle with many unanswered questions about her background, her life and her new-found faith. Slowly but surely she began to look beyond her immediate situation and, after four months, she asked if it would be possible to leave the red-light area.

It has been nine years since Zarine left the brothels. Today she is unrecognizable from the girl we first met. Those nine years have been full of both pain and joy as she has slowly but surely rebuilt her life on the rock of God's love for her. When she first came out we arranged for her to stay with a family who we thought would create the kind of welcoming atmosphere that she needed, but they couldn't cope with her HIV-positive status and so, once more, she was rejected. Then she went to our newly established community for women and children who had been ostracized because of their HIV status. There, through the love, counsel and training she received, she began to put the pieces of her life back together. A lot happened over the following few years, but eventually she decided that she wanted to give her life to helping others who had been trafficked into prostitution. And so for the past seven years she has served on our staff doing exactly that. Of course she is the best equipped to fulfil that role because, unlike the other staff members, she knows and understands the trauma these girls face on a daily basis. She also understands their internal struggles as they contemplate leaving the only community they know. For us, one of the greatest joys is to see someone who has been discarded, rejected, traumatized, and placed at the bottom of the pile of humanity not only begin the path to wholeness, but also give her life to work that others might be whole too. Zarine is one of those.

Personal Freedom

I wish I could tell you that every one of those girls in the brothels who has the opportunity to begin again chooses that path. I wish I could tell you that every street child who has the opportunity to come off the streets chooses to do so. I wish I could tell you that every child addicted to solvents, when given an opportunity to join a detoxification programme, chooses to go that route. I wish I could tell you that everyone who experiences God's overwhelming love for them chooses to follow him. But, as you know, unfortunately they don't. And, what's more, there is nothing that you and I can do about it. No amount of force, manipulation or cajoling will make a difference because *change comes from within*.

Many of us wish we had a greater ability to influence others. Many parents wish that they could somehow control their children's behaviour; many children wish they could make their parents understand their point of view. In the church, people wish that they could just force someone to accept Christ and live out his or her life based on the truth that they have discovered. But it doesn't work like that. And it doesn't work like that because God has made the universe to work on a different basis – that of individuality and free choice. As G.C. Berkouwer, in the midst of a discussion on determinism, says,

> We must then speak without hesitation of human freedom as a creaturely freedom given by God. No misuse of the desire for freedom, not even complete anarchy, should tempt us to stop speaking boldly and emphatically of freedom.[2]

The fact that we are made in the image of God means that we have personal freedom and choice. Even though this freedom may be curtailed through the force exerted on an individual's external environment, no one is able to demand internal change, belief, love or respect. Because *all* people have been made in God's image – not some, not a few, not the majority, but *all* people – all are in control of their own internal world. And it is in this internal world that a person decides to change. Yes, change truly comes from within. While you can force a person into showing a sign of respect, to bow or kneel, for example, that does not mean you are achieving respect itself. Respect is an internal attitude and, though behaviour can be forced, attitude cannot.

Those who work among the poor learn very quickly that this principle will both test and develop them as people. From the point of view of the outsider, the issues that street children face appear to be so simple to resolve. But the view from the inside is very different. There are attitudes, expectations, issues of trust and loyalty to work through, and past traumas to overcome. And so you might just need to be patient for ten years to see a handful come through. God doesn't seem to be in a hurry, and it's important for us to remember the benefits of his patience. When we look at our own lives, we value the way God is patient with us. We are humbled by, and grateful for, how he works with us cooperatively in the process of change and does not force his way on us. For some reason it's tempting to adopt a different attitude when it comes to others. Any of us who yearn to see God's transformation in our lives or in the lives of others just have to be patient.

Many of those who have lived lives of destitute poverty and whose lives have become utterly fragmented can be restored to wholeness, but it will take time – a lot of time. Just learning to trust someone is like learning to walk all over again. A person who lives with no steady, meaningful and trusting relationship in their lives for years on end becomes disconnected with life as you and I know it. That person will only learn to trust through the patient, steadfast, loving care that you provide in your relationship with them. This is real empowerment – the relational exchange between you and another person. Though it may seem simplistic, relationships between people are at the heart of any project – relationships between staff members who possess a holistic and integrated mindset and those they serve. Although the skills that people learn, the education they receive, the bandages for their wounds and the food that nourishes malnourished bodies are all important, change will come through relational empowerment. God can, and occasionally does, radically change some people in an instant. God can, and occasionally does, radically change some people in isolation, outside of relationships with others. But these are the exceptions. The vast majority of people are changed, over a considerable period of time, through the relationships they have.

Angela was ten years old when she came to Oasis to escape the abuse she was suffering at the hands of the woman for whom she worked. Her parents and siblings had all died, and her grandmother had arranged for her to live with this woman in order that she could go to school in the city. Angela's grandmother did not know that she was actually working as a housemaid and was never sent to school. When Angela first came to Oasis she found it incredibly difficult to trust anyone, so her story was always changing and it was hard to know what the truth really was. She went to live in a halfway facility set up for homeless women in Kampala. There she was cared for and loved and, gradually, she began to trust other people. One thing she did not want to do, though, was ever return to her grandmother. After every other girl at this halfway facility was resettled, Angela remained – she needed more time. One of our staff members decided to foster her until she was ready. Other staff went through the difficult procedure of trying to trace her grandmother. Through the love and concern shown for her at this foster home Angela grew and developed. She was a natural leader and even became head girl of her school. In time arrangements were made for a visit to her grandmother, and then another one, just to see if reconciliation was possible. It took time, but eventually Angela made the decision to return and live with her grandmother, whom she had grown to love through the reconciliation process. It was her decision, and she made it in her time. Had she been forced to return before she was ready, true reconciliation might never have taken place.

Force Never Works

The history of Christianity is, unfortunately, replete with examples of Christians forcing their faith on others. It has never worked. People live out their lives based not on what they say they believe, but rather on what they truly believe. A person can recite a statement of faith either by free choice or through force, but the reality of whether they believe it or not can only be seen by how they live. Someone who recites the Lord's Prayer but does not forgive their neighbour shows by this behaviour where their true belief lies. While it is important to set high expectations and, in group settings, to have rules that all abide by, we cannot force someone to do something or become something that they do not want to do or become.

The Oasis staff have followed through on this principle in work among girls who have been trafficked into prostitution. Initially, when we began a small project in the heart of Mumbai's red-light area, our approach was to build relationships with the girls as well as with the madams and see where it would take us. In our hearts, of course, we longed for girls to experience a new life outside the brothels, and we set up a process and a safe environment where they would be cared for when they did leave. These girls we worked amongst were girls over the age of eighteen who had some measure of freedom to leave (in contrast to the minors we also work to free). We soon found out, however, that it is a painful thing to provide an open door and watch as people turn and walk in the other direction.

Sharmila's story

Here is an extract from an interview with Sharmila, one of the girls with whom Oasis works as part of the Aruna project in Mumbai. The interview was recently conducted by Clare Nonhebel, who spent time at the project when visiting from the UK. Manju, one of our staff, acted as interpreter.

Sharmila begins, 'I was married and I have a little girl who is six years old.

'My husband was in a terrorist group and planted bombs. He never listened to me. I begged him to stop, but he went on with it. He lost all the flesh from both legs in a bomb blast and was admitted to hospital, then moved to another hospital far away.

'The baby was very small so it was hard for me. I sold all the land and the animals I had, and my gold, and I got work in the farmhouse – very hard work – to get money, because my husband was ill.

'I had a friend who worked in Mumbai who promised me a good job. She said, "I will give you some housework and you can do a beautician's course." I said no, because of my baby, and the lady said, "You can come with your baby and work, with your baby."

'So I came to Mumbai with my baby and stayed the first night in a hotel and the second night in a building I thought was a hotel, but there was a lot of noise in the night and I couldn't work out what was going on and when I woke up in the morning, everyone was sleeping. Then I understood what kind of a place it was.'

'I found I had been sold for 50,000 rupees,' Sharmila resumes. 'When evening came, the women were all getting ready and the men were coming to the door. And they told me to get ready and put on make-up and I said no; I wouldn't sit down with them.

'I was there 15 days. I was not willing, so the madam told me to go to another house; she said I would live as family there and I would like that place better.

'The madam told the pimps to take me to this second place, but one of the girls told me the pimps were planning to sell me off for one lakh and said I would never get out then.'

A lakh is 100,000 rupees, about $2,000 – a huge sum of money for a girl to pay off. The girl who tipped Sharmila off was probably right – it would take a lifetime to pay back if the pimps resold her for that amount. The money the girls are entitled to keep for themselves is held back from them until the 'debt' is paid, when they're free to leave the brothel – in theory. In the meantime they are given or loaned small amounts, but Manju says the girls tend to spend the money as soon as they have any.

'The madam had given me her number "in case there were any problems",' Sharmila continues, 'so I went out to phone her and say I was in a bad place. I thought she was trying to help me. But she didn't trust the pimps; that's why she gave me the number. She was angry with them because she had one plan and they had another – to make money for themselves and not her – so they got a beating.

'I didn't realize that they all knew each other and this second place was the same thing; it looked as though we lived as a family – but when the phone calls came, the women had to go.'

There's still no expression in her face or in her voice. She recounts the story of her second deception and sale as though it's beyond emotion.

'The manager used to drink and beat the girls, and took my child and put her in care. They said I could see her but they never allowed me to go downstairs out of the building. They said, "When you are clear of your debt, you can go out."

Still no sign of emotion. She's very still, very controlled. There's no need for Manju or me to prompt her with questions.

'During this time, my husband rang the police from the hospital and said this lady had taken me to Mumbai. The police found my baby in the hostel and asked where the mother was, and the manager said they didn't know the mother, but the police said, "How did the baby get here, then?" and threatened to arrest the manager, so he gave them the phone number.

'The police called the brothel and said my child was not well and I should come soon, so the madam told me just to go and see the child and come back, and sent the boy from the brothel with me, but when we arrived the police asked him to take them to the place where I had been staying and they arrested them.'

This is different from the other women's stories: the first time I've heard about the police doing anything about this people-trafficking. It sounds encouraging.

'I stayed two days in the police station and had a medical check-up, then I went back to my home,' Sharmila says. 'The police back home wanted me to tell them everything, and the whole gang got caught and were given three months in jail.'

Three months doesn't sound a particularly heavy sentence for selling a woman to be raped every night and for taking her baby away.

'But they were wealthy people and they paid money and came out,' Sharmila says.

'They didn't even serve the three months?'

'No.'

'Bribes,' Manju explains.

Sharmila still shows no expression except resignation.

'My husband was willing to take me back,' she goes on, 'but my mother-in-law was asking questions about where I'd been, and there was gossip. I stayed one year but there was a lot of pain. My husband listened to his mother and started calling me names and then he divorced me. He still wasn't working, and there was no money to bring up my child, and everyone was saying bad things about me.

'So I left my child with my mother at home and just came back to Mumbai. I earned 70,000 rupees while I was in Mumbai but the boy from the brothel who had been in prison told me I had to repay the money. After six months I left but they didn't give me the full amount I'd earned, so that I'd have to come back for the rest of my money, and when I went home again I found my house was empty; everything had been taken.'

I can see why she said her story is a long one. Just when everything that could happen has happened, it gets worse. And then worse.

Still no emotion. The only sign of upheaval is that every now and again she carefully refolds the pleat of her scarf and settles it more neatly, with its ends flipped back over her shoulders.

'While I was in the brothel I fell in love with a boy who said he'd take me home to my native place and marry me, so I thought my life would change now. I got married and we went back and I gave my new husband the 50,000 rupees I had, but within three months he and his mother were giving me trouble. They didn't give me food or water and they told me they didn't want my child.'

And worse.

'So I went back to my mother's place. I was with my mother one year and my husband never called me or came back for me. I worked at making cigarettes but it was very little money. There wasn't enough for food and clothes and I had to take care of my child. So I told my mother, "I'll go out and make some money and come back," and my mother was crying.'

I feel God was probably crying as well.

'I came back to Mumbai and earned one more lakh and a good customer told me to put the money into a scheme and I took his advice. I got some land and also put some money in the bank for my daughter.

'My mother wanted to file against the second husband for divorce because he never came back.'

'Did you want a divorce?' I ask her.

'I told her to do what she thought best. She contacted his family and they said he had gone abroad, but he came back and called me, so I went back to him. Then he went abroad again and I didn't know if he would come back and keep me as a wife.'

Waiting for her mother to decide about the divorce, and her husband to decide if he wanted her.

'What do you want?' I ask.

She doesn't seem sure what to answer. Perhaps she can't imagine being given the choice, or thinks that whatever she chose would be impossible to attain.

I put the question another way. 'What would you like God to do for you? How shall I pray for you, when I leave here?'

'I am worried about my girl – if she grows up and knows about me,' Sharmila says. 'I have this land and I want to build a house but I have to make some more money. I could do some other work if I could get a good job, to keep us.'

It sounds like an impossible dream, all right. She's only just learning to read and write, and where would she get a reference for this good job?

'How do you feel about your life?' I ask Sharmila.

I haven't yet heard her say how she feels about anything. The answer is swift and heartfelt – a different tone from the rest of her narrative.

'I don't like to do this dirty work.'

Something has changed here. It feels as though something has snapped.

'Can I just say . . . ?' I ask Manju, but she's standing up and her face says she's had enough. She has taken a lot of the strain of this afternoon, emotionally and spiritually, as well as the mental effort of interpreting. But I need to say this to Sharmila.

So I say it to her face, in English, even knowing she doesn't speak a word of it.

'You've done so much,' I tell her. 'You've tried so hard to put things right, over and over again. Do you think it's time just to receive now? To let people help you?'

Sharmila starts crying. She clenches her fists in an effort to stop.

She turns to Manju and gestures incomprehension. Manju, bless her, sits down again and translates the words. Sharmila is now crying even more. I go and fetch my bag and give her a packet of tissues. Manju takes one out and hands it to her.

'Would she be willing to let me pray with her?' I ask.

'I think so,' Manju says. 'I'll stay and pray too.'

'Only if she's OK with it.'

She asks and Sharmila says yes.

Haneefa and Rupa are sitting quietly at the end of the room. I call them over and ask them to help us pray. Manju sits and holds Sharmila's hands, while the other three of us stand.

I don't want to pray in silence: it means the only sound will be Sharmila sobbing and that would embarrass her. Praying aloud in English would mean Manju has to go on interpreting, or no one would understand a word, and she's tired.

So I pray in tongues, which is a way of letting God's Spirit take over, using whatever words or sounds happen to come to mind. That way we're even: nobody understands a word except God, who after all is the only one who can do anything in this impossible situation.

I pray till Sharmila's stopped crying and she has gone very still. We sit down and wait for her to come back to herself. After a while she gets up and hugs me, then Manju, then without saying a word she goes out.

Across the street, back to the brothel.

It's such a short step.

And such a long journey to make in the opposite direction.

Will Sharmila manage to break the cords and go free? God only knows.[3]

Our role is not to judge

Some of these girls have chosen to stay and some have left, but we need to remember that, for those girls who do stay, there is still time and opportunity to make the break. God's compassion for them in the distress and complexity of their situations is not dependent on their response, and neither must our compassion have any strings attached. Our role is to love, help, encourage and advocate; we must refrain from judging; we must never force what we want; we must remain constant in the whirlwind of their lives. Our role is to constantly and consistently tell them that God is on their side, that he gave his life that they may experience life in all its fullness, that there truly is hope, however hopeless their situation might appear to be.

Some of you reading this might wonder why these girls struggle with the possibility of leaving, and it is a complex question. Many of these girls have been living this way for years and often they have lost all contact with their families. Many feel incredible shame and know they would not be welcome back home anyway. Often they find that their only relationships and community are in the brothels with other girls who are in similar situations. They have an incredible amount to gain by leaving, but it's an enormous risk to enter the unknown world outside while potentially losing the only community they have. The decision always has to be theirs. And, slowly but surely, some have made that decision and have left the only community they have ever really known to set out on the long, painful but ultimately fulfilling path to wholeness.

Jesus' Approach

It is fascinating to watch how, when Jesus dealt with people, he didn't feel he had to tie everything down. He never forced people into making decisions and he left loads of room for people to find their way in their own time to the place of understanding or commitment. Take, for example, the time when a group of men brought their paralytic friend to Jesus in the hope that he could be healed. Jesus told the unnamed individual that his sins were forgiven and then entered into conversation with the religious leaders who thought he was blaspheming. He then told the paralytic to get up and go home, which he did – no lecture, no sermon, no challenge to commitment, no altar call. Jesus simply let the man and his friends return home[4]

It's freeing for us to know that, when we engage in conversation with a stranger, we don't need to lead that discussion to one particular place – as some of the older models of evangelism taught us. Rather, we can be free to engage as a fellow traveller, knowing that what we share can play its part in the wider picture of the other person's life. Instead of trying to force or manipulate, worrying that it is all up to us to challenge a person in case they get hit by a bus tomorrow, we can actually approach other people with greater faith as we trust that it is God who puts the pieces together, often in ways we don't understand. As Henri Nouwen reminds us,

> Jesus cared deeply for the people he met. He did not control or dominate them, but through his words and actions offered them an opportunity to search for new directions and make new choices.[5]

Jesus' approach was so different from the way some Christians approach people today with their emphasis on saving souls and getting people into heaven. Jesus never employed the tactic of praying 'the sinner's prayer'. He seemed much more concerned with the situations in which people found themselves in the present than with their eternal futures. His emphasis was on experiencing God now, today, in their lives. Jesus doesn't seem to have any of that 'I need to force a conversation here because it might be the only time this person will hear the gospel' stuff. Instead he appears to approach his work in a much more relaxed way, seemingly aware that issues of eternal destiny are worked out in time and are not simply dependent on whether he makes the most of every opportunity. And, what is more, his approach to

sharing truth relies far more on people's responses than
it does on telling people straight what they 'need to
know'. Jesus even explained that this was why he spoke
in parables – so that those who really wanted to follow
could understand while those who didn't want to, or
who weren't ready, were shielded from understanding.
As Brian McLaren reminds us,

> If it's the heart that counts, then hearts cannot be coerced;
> nobody can be forced. They can be invited, attracted,
> intrigued, enticed, and challenged – but not forced. And
> that is perhaps the greatest genius of a parable: it doesn't
> grab you by the lapels and scream in your face, 'Repent,
> you vile sinner! Turn or burn!' Rather, it works gently, sub-
> tly, indirectly. It respects your dignity. It doesn't batter you
> into submission but leaves you free to discover and choose
> for yourself.[6]

Jesus never demands faith from anyone; he simply
acknowledges it's there. We can see that in the incident
with the paralytic mentioned above. He didn't tell the
person to have faith; he saw that it was there and
acknowledged it.[7] How different this is from the
approach of some who believe that they need to help
people see what great sinners they are in order to help
them come to a place of faith. Please don't misunderstand me – I am not saying that we shouldn't be 'evangelical' and share our faith with others. I believe we
should. Neither am I denying the reality of sin or saying
that people shouldn't pray a prayer of commitment. I am
simply questioning the approach that some in the
Christian community take. Interestingly, when Jesus did
enter into lengthy discourses with people – as he did
with both Nicodemus[8] and the Samaritan woman[9] – it
was not because he had an agenda he was trying to get

across. Rather, the lengthy conversations flowed from the questions these people continued to ask him.

Many of the poor don't need to be told that they are sinners. The homeless, street children, women working as prostitutes, those living in urban slums – these folk often know that they are in need of God's forgiveness and love. We don't need to convince them of their sin. What they often need to be convinced of instead is their value. For when a person has been ostracized and marginalized it is easy for them to believe in their own worthlessness. It is the truth of Genesis 1, and not the truth of Genesis 3, that is hard for them to comprehend.

In his wonderful book *The Jesus I Never Knew* Philip Yancey picks up on what Ivan Karamazov called 'the miracle of restraint'[10] – the fact that God chooses not to force his way on us, those who have been made in his image. Even when we ignore or reject him God still does not use force to get our attention, though of course he could. Instead, God waits and loves and longs for our response knowing, as Yancey points out, that 'only love can summon a response of love'. As Yancey reflects on this in the light of his own upbringing, he echoes the experience of many others I know today who still struggle with the forceful approach that their churches espouse.

This quality of restraint in Jesus – one could almost call it a divine shyness – took me by surprise. I realized, as I absorbed the story of Jesus in the Gospels, that I had expected from him the same qualities I had met in the southern fundamentalist church of my childhood. There, I often felt the victim of emotional pressures. Doctrine was dished out in a 'Believe and don't ask questions!' style. Wielding the power of miracle, mystery, and authority, the church left no place for doubt. I also learned manipulative techniques for 'soul-winning,' some of which involved misrepresenting myself to the person I was talking to. Yet now I am unable to find any of these qualities in the life of Jesus.[11]

One of the saddest things for those of us who were on the Oasis staff was to see how some reacted when the people who had come to faith through our work joined a local congregation. We did, of course, encourage people to join a local church where they would be welcomed and nurtured. Sadly, though, some churches made it abundantly clear to newcomers from the streets and brothels that there was a limited time frame in which they were expected to shape up. Some people see transformation as a six- to twelve-month process! How very different that is from the way God works with us. How patient God is with me as I battle with some of the same issues that I've been battling for thirty years or more. Surely the way that God works with me should be reflected in the way I approach and encourage other people.

One consequence of understanding that all people are made in God's image will be a respect for the personal freedom and choice of those who are disenfranchised, poor and marginalized – the personal freedom and choice God gives each one of us. Because we understand this truth we will choose not to force ourselves, or our views, on them. We will choose not to manipulate situations in order to elicit the response we want from them. We will choose to continue to be there for them when they make choices that take them far from where we would want them to be and, we believe, from where God would want them to be. We will choose the path of weakness rather than that of strength.

If relational empowerment is vital for change to occur in people's lives, then we need to factor that into the structures and systems we put in place in our organizations and programmes. When rigid job descriptions that

are task-oriented dictate what people do, people will not
be empowered. The project may have structure and it
may be specialized in its delivery, but if relationships
that empower those served are not developed then we
are missing the most vital component of all. The most
important thing a street child or an unemployed young
person from the slums receives from our interaction with
them is a vision for their future – of what it could be like,
of who they can become, of the potential they can fulfil.
We need to work with people at the level of their dreams,
hopes and desires. When a street child learns to read and
write it is an amazing accomplishment, but when that
child tells you, 'I want to be a teacher', it is even better.
When a girl from the brothels learns to cut a pattern and
stitch a dress that is great, but when she tells you, 'I want
to be the best tailor in town', it is even better. And it is
better because they have a hope, a dream and picture of
what the future might be.

Such hope doesn't come overnight – it emerges over
time as someone begins to see him or herself differently.
And people see themselves differently only when they
learn to do this through relationship. People who have
been rejected for certain behaviours in the past will often
repeat those behaviours in new relationships. But when
you develop a relationship with a person and repeatedly refuse to reject that person, and when it finally
dawns on them that you are not going to reject them
regardless of what they did or do, they come to trust
you. And, slowly, they will begin to see themselves differently as you reflect a different person back. Of course,
most people know also that their dreams and visions for
the future are so impossible that they cannot get there
alone. They know that it is only with God's help that
they will be able to fulfil those dreams and be who they
desire to be. They know that if they cooperate with God

> Because all people are made in the image of God, we respect that all people must make their own decisions about who they want to be. Each individual must plot his or her own path. We choose not to force our way on the poor, but rather we come to support, encourage, and cheer from the sidelines — knowing that change comes from within.

and follow his leading then God can take the brokenness of their past and mould something of incredible value. And God does not disappoint. Everything will probably not be straightforward, and everything might not work out exactly the way one imagines, but God has arms open wide to help those who are poor fulfil their dreams and realize the potential that God put in them in the first place. The only trouble God has is that he has to convince us to be his hands and feet in the process.

6

Empowerment

Agents of transformation are people willing to come alongside those with needs to educate and empower them. This
will transform hearts, minds, lives and communities.
— *Richard Starcher*[1]

Janet is a single mother of five children who lives in a desperately poor slum community in the city of Mbale in the
east of Uganda. Without any form of regular income, she
could not afford to send her children to school or even find
enough food to feed them.
They would often eat only
one meal a day, made up of
the 'rice waste' that most
people would throw away.
HIV has taken a heavy toll
in the community in which
Janet lives, as it has in much
of the rest of the country.
This means not only that
there are many single mothers but that there are some
child-headed families as
well. The main source of

> Because all people are made in the
> image of God, all people have
> inherent dignity. We respect the
> dignity of the poor as human
> beings who possess the same
> capacity that we have. We do not,
> therefore, come to them thinking
> that we know what they need and
> then give it to them. Rather, we
> come to them seeking to empower
> them to be in control of their own
> lives, choices and destiny.

income for many who live there comes from the brewing of homemade liquor, and the stench from fermentation is overwhelming. The knock-on effect of this is a high degree of alcoholism, even among children. Children as young as seven years old are recruited to work in brewing.

Two of Janet's children became involved in a six-month programme that Oasis ran in that community for those who needed either to catch up in their education in order to gain school admission or who were beyond that and needed basic life skills to enable them to get jobs. As our staff developed a relationship with Janet they asked her about her hopes and dreams for the future, for herself as well as for her children. Janet wanted to work but needed something that she could do from her home. She was adamant about not getting involved in brewing because of the impact she could see that it had in the lives of so many in the community. Over the course of several discussions we learned that one thing Janet wanted to be able to do was to use her weaving skills which she had learnt many years previously. Her problem was that she didn't know how to go about selling anything she might produce. Our staff suggested that if she was able to begin weaving again they could work with her on a basic marketing strategy and provide the very small capital investment she required to begin. A year and a half later Janet has a thriving business that provides an income sufficient for all her children to attend school and eat good, healthy, regular meals. More than that, despite the many challenges she still faces, as Janet lies down to sleep at night she has a deep sense of fulfilment that she is able to provide for herself and her family.

Janet's story is a story of empowerment. It is a story of someone who has taken authority over the circumstances of her own life, who has decided that the answer lies within and not in someone else's solution. Sometimes all it takes is a conversation. Other times it takes years, but the turning point is always when someone begins to believe in him or herself, in who they are, in their capacity. The role that we then take is to come alongside as a helper, an encourager, a facilitator. Sometimes people may need some training or practical assistance, but that is only useful after they have turned that corner and perceive such assistance as helping them to achieve their goals. Empowerment is the place of weakness, not the place of strength. It is the opposite of telling people what to do or providing what you think they need.

Ernesto Sirolli has written a wonderful book called *Ripples from the Zambezi* in which he outlines the approach he took to economic development among poor communities. Sirolli explains how he hung out in communities waiting for people to take the initiative in seeking out his assistance and how he played the role of assisting them to do what they wanted to do – not what he thought was best for them or their community. The book exudes empowerment and is a great read. He crystallizes his message as follows,

> Right now, in your community, at this very moment, there is someone who is dreaming about doing something to improve his/her lot. If we could learn how to help that person transform the dream into meaningful work, we would be halfway to changing the economic fortunes of the entire community.[2]

We can sometimes get the impression that poverty can be made history through big plans and schemes. In his book *The White Man's Burden*,[3] William Easterly demonstrates how naïve that view really is as he contrasts the approach of the 'planners' with that of the 'searchers'. His views are based on the reality that, despite all the major campaigns and government targets to eliminate poverty, we still can't get twelve-cent medicines to children with malaria. The planners, he says, come from outside and have the solutions already in mind. The searchers admit they don't have the answers but realize that solutions come from inside a community. The planners have big targets and propose large-scale solutions, while searchers work from the grass roots up. Both planners and searchers can be well-meaning, compassionate people who long for change. But only searchers understand that long-lasting and sustainable change occurs as people are empowered to make a difference in their own lives, families, and communities.

All People Possess an Inbuilt Need to Contribute

Work is very important. If a person is able to secure a job, he or she can address some of the economic issues of poverty – but that is only one aspect of work's importance. Perhaps even more important is the fact that employment provides people with the opportunity to play their part as 'stewards of the earth' – the mandate given to humankind in Genesis 2. Somehow, our sense of worth and value is wrapped up in making a contribution – and work is the key way that we do that. This is, I believe, a reflection of being made in God's image. And since all people have been made in God's image, all people have that inbuilt need to make a contribution.

When someone is able to earn an income to support their family they feel a sense of worth as they fulfil a key responsibility. It is an outworking of the principle 'it is more blessed to give than to receive'. Such a principle is written on our hearts as human beings. This is not something that is only relevant to the exchange of gifts – it is a natural outworking of being made in the image of a giving, loving, sacrificial God. When we deny people the opportunity to make a contribution, in whatever shape or form that might take, we deny them the right to be human and to fulfil their God-given mandate. This is why volunteering is a key concept in society. People want to volunteer because they want to make a contribution. Often people volunteer in the social realm because they do not feel that they are making a contribution through their work, even though the money they earn may be more than sufficient for their needs.

Unfortunately, sometimes the system we create robs people of this opportunity to make a contribution and of the dignity that comes from fulfilling who we were created to be. Robert Lupton has some harsh things to say about the welfare system in the United States.

Take people who are able and strong. Place them in the wealthiest land on earth. Surround them with unparalleled opportunity. Then pay them not to work, not to strive, not to achieve. Pay them to accept nonproductivity as a way of life. Agree to subsidize their families with food, shelter, health care, and money if the fathers will leave.

Do this for two or three generations and see what you produce. You will have a people who are unmotivated and dependent, whose hopes and dreams rise no higher than their subsidies – a people who have lost the work ethic, who have learned that others will take responsibility for them and who therefore assert little discipline or control over their own lives. You will have emasculated their men, making them expendable and unnecessary to their families' existence. You will have created a generation of prideless, fatherless youth who believe that receiving and taking is

better than working and investing. And when you have
seen the hope disappear from the eyes of the young, you
can be sure you have developed an effective formula for the
destruction of a people. We call it welfare.[4]

When our family left Mumbai and moved to another
mega-city in another part of the world, we got involved
in a large and thriving church there with fantastic worship, great teaching and friendly people. Once a month
the church ran a feeding programme in one of the most
deprived parts of the city and we, as a family, got
involved in helping with that. Around eight thirty in the
morning we would meet up at the church and pray
together before going down to the community in convoy.
One or two of the leaders had already done the work of
loading a large truck with groceries that was then driven
down to a school compound in the community. When we
arrived we would sort the food that was already on large
palettes and lay it all out in the playground in a couple of
lines. Those who would benefit were already beginning
to arrive by the time we got there, but they were asked to
line up in an orderly fashion outside the fence. The gate
was kept shut until all the food was unloaded and ready
to be distributed. By about ten thirty there would be close
to 70 people waiting, all with their shopping trolleys that
at some point previously had ended up as household
property. Inside we were each assigned a palette and
stood by it, lifting one or two of the items we had into the
trolleys of those who came. After going all the way down
the line, people were ushered out through the building
where their only obligation was to receive a short individual prayer of blessing from those who had chosen that
to be their role instead of the food distribution.

The people who ran this were good people, but it
was one of the most disempowering experiences I have

witnessed in my life. I tried to talk with the leaders about alternative ways to help address the needs of that community, but to no avail. This was my plan. Since this community needed and wanted a cheap supply of food, and since people in the church had managed to persuade some wholesalers to provide certain produce free of charge, I suggested that we simply act as brokers. The community could elect a group from among themselves to run a cheap food distribution programme. It could even be a small business for someone from the community to run. We could then broker a relationship between the food companies and that community group, and they could sell the food they received at highly discounted prices – either to cover the costs of transportation or to make a small income for whoever was doing the work. That way the community would be in control of the programme, they would be doing something to meet their own needs and, most important of all, their dignity would remain intact. Sadly, the leaders of the programme were not in a place to think of running the programme a different way.

Empowering Communities

Empowerment is worked out at both an individual and community level. When we provide something for a community we are in control; it is a client-provider relationship and people either receive it or they don't. When we work alongside people we do more than provide something: we draw out what is in them; we help them take control of their own destiny; we focus on their capacity, not their deficiency. It is better for them and better for us. I sometimes wonder whether some of the programmes that churches and organizations run are set

up for the benefit of those who run them. I am not argu-
ing against feeding the hungry and clothing the naked,
for in many parts of the world such relief is essential.
Rather, it is important to understand how easy it is to
disempower people who are not in need of relief.

Empowerment begins with listening. It begins with
asking questions and ascertaining where people are at
and what their hopes are. Empowerment is responsive
rather than prescriptive. It does not take a response in
one context and automatically transpose it to another. As
Richard Starcher says, in reflecting on the concept of
transformational development,

> Transformational development must take seriously the cul-
> tural context of the society in transformation. If it doesn't, it
> represents domination rather than transformation. Context-
> ualization is achieved by humbly listening to those who
> know their own local environment. The helper must first be
> a listener.[5]

Let me share a few examples of what empowerment might
look like in a community setting. One community in which
Oasis works in Mumbai, India is made up of a variety of
different groups that all came to the city in search of a better future. Five thousand families are crammed together
within a couple of square miles. Research conducted six
years previously had found that the community identified
the usual issues as key areas of concern: lack of education
for the children; unsanitary conditions; health-related
problems; and debt. Each of these could be addressed by
providing a service – health clinics, loan schemes, schooling, and so on. And it is always a huge temptation to go
this route. If we did this, however, we would be the people
in control, the people in power. It would be a relationship
that could so easily lead to dependency.

The unsanitary conditions were one of the first concerns to be addressed in that slum community. The open drainage system made diseases, and especially skin infections, much more prevalent. Replacing it with a covered system would make a considerable difference. Our role, though, was not to do the work or to raise the money, but simply to help the community do what it wanted to do. Kuldeep, who was the Oasis project leader there, chatted with one of the key community leaders about the situation and made the suggestion that the local government minister might be willing to help. He then brokered a meeting, and the result was that the local government provided the materials, the community provided the labour and, over time, lane by lane, the whole of the community built a covered drainage system for themselves. Since then there has been a 90% decrease in the cases of skin infection.

Another key issue in this community was that 70% of the people were in debt to loan sharks, the only source of capital that people in the slum could access. It was a profitable business for someone who had money to lend to those who could not access banking facilities. The going rate was between 40% and 50% APR. Of course, people didn't realize how much interest they were being charged because those who set up the loans only spoke about the weekly or monthly payment that seemed so small compared to the total being borrowed. And loan sharks were the only option for those in financial crisis who could not borrow the money from others in their family. Again, our role was not to become a bank for them but to empower them to enter the existing banking system. In practice what happened was that small women's savings groups were formed, made up of ten to fifteen ladies each. Those groups then elected their own leader and secretary. Initially there were just two groups, but as each of these women put aside Rs20 (30 pence) per week the amount soon added up. Collectively, then, they were able to approach the bank since they had more than the minimum amount that was required to open an account. When a person then needed a loan, they were able to take money from the collective amount that had been deposited – thereby creating a community bank within the wider banking system. Loans were given out at an interest rate of 8%. Slowly but surely, each person who had been trapped in a debt cycle with the loan sharks managed to pay off their outstanding amount. Now there are over four hundred women involved in 32 groups operating as a registered federation with a president elected by them. This is community owned, community run, and for the benefit of those within the community. In fact, what has happened is that these groups are now able to address a far broader range of issues as a collective voice. One person can always be ignored, the federation as a whole cannot be ignored. Some of the activities that are run in the community include a pre-school, a computer training facility and a tailoring course. Each of these activities is organized and run by the local community for themselves. An empowerment approach looks completely different from the provision of services.

One of the issues in another community where Oasis works was that there were many teenage boys who had dropped out of school at an early age. They didn't work and spent their time either gambling what little money they had or creating trouble for others. They were repeating a cycle that they had seen modelled by others – it was a trap from which they couldn't escape. One day, one of our staff members was in conversation with a group of boys and discovered that they had an interest in football. He then arranged for them to meet up early in the morning on a small football pitch next to the railway line and within walking distance of their slum. They enjoyed the football so much that permission was sought to use the ground on a regular basis. Before long, thirty teenagers were turning out every weekday morning at six thirty for training. A new football team was born.

This initiative had several important results. First, the boys involved now had an outlet for their pent-up energy that they could direct towards a purposeful activity. Second, they began to learn about some basic life disciplines, including timekeeping and teamwork. Third, as they developed their abilities they felt a sense of achievement – something that most of them had never experienced in the education system. This lack of achievement had actually been one of the key reasons many of them had dropped out of school in the first place. Over the course of their time together each of the boys began to have conversations with the coaches about their lives, their hopes for the future and the pos-sibility of either re-entering the education system or get-ting a job. A lot of these conversations happened over a cup of chai immediately after the early morning training was over. Each of these teenagers was different, but as they began to express some measure of hope for their futures our role was simply to facilitate their achieve-ment of their own goals. This is what empowerment is really about – assisting people to be who they want to be and do what they want to do.

One of the boys who joined the football training was Ramu. He had dropped out of school and began to mix with the wrong company and spent a lot of his time drink-ing and gambling. His parents were understandably concerned, but the disgrace this brought on his family prompted them to suggest that he leave home – an unus-ual request in Indian culture. When Ramu started attend-ing the training sessions he wasn't really serious about getting fit or developing his skills. He came because he didn't have anything else to do and he enjoyed the camaraderie of the others who attended. Over time, though, it finally dawned on him that he had a gift for playing and that if he worked on his fitness and practised, then he could go a long way. Ramu set his heart on playing football professionally and so began to take his training seriously. As he pursued this goal, other things began to fall into place for him. He started studying again and relationships with his family were restored. After a couple of years of training Ramu got a chance to represent his state at the under-eighteen level and was then selected for an all-India training camp. He continues to pursue his goal of playing at a professional level in the future.

God Empowers

Empowerment is biblical. In the Old Testament, as a response to the emergence of poverty in Israel, God commanded the people not to harvest to the very edge of their fields but to leave some of the crop unharvested so that the poor could glean what remained.[6] As Esteban Voth points out, gleaning was work and reflected an approach to poverty that empowered people to do something about their situation instead of relying on charity.[7] As such it preserved people's dignity which, as we have said, stands in stark contrast to the welfare system of the United States and some other Western countries. Dewi Hughes points out that the same principle lay behind the Sabbath of the land instituted on a seven-year cycle,[8] as well as the laws about lending money to those who were in need.

A loan constituted an opportunity for poor persons to use their strength and ingenuity to provide for themselves and in so doing to express their dignity as human beings created to be workers in God's world. This explains the strong repudiation of interest and usury in the Old Testament. In the community of God's people Israel, the rich were to supply freely the means for the poor to work themselves out of poverty.[9]

When our starting point is that all people have been made in the image of God, we will look at people in terms of their capacity instead of their deficiency. Service systems are built on the premise that people are deficient. John McKnight has categorized capacity and deficiency and argues that the focus on 'services' replaced our focus on the production of 'goods' because of the need to keep the economy growing.[10] Whether or not that is true, there is a clear connection between seeing people as deficient and providing a service. Myers backs this up by saying, 'If poverty is the absence of things, then the solution is to provide them. This often leads to the outside becoming the development "Santa Claus," bringing all good things: food, well drilling, education, and proclamation. The poor are seen as passive recipients, incomplete human beings we make complete and whole through our largess.'[11]

Our paradigm of poverty needs to change. As long as we see the poor in terms of deficiency we will be unable to address the real issues, which are alienation and exclusion. It is not that the poor are deficient, it is that so often they are unable to make choices to impact their future. They are disempowered.

Seeing People's Capacity, not Their Deficiency

Empowerment, as we have seen, is about seeing people's capacity, not their deficiency. It emerges from a belief that, because all people have been made in God's image, all people possess the ability to dream, plan, create, love, give and contribute. This is why we do not work among the poor to provide them with that which they do not have in order that they can have a better future. Rather, we work among the poor to help them build a better future through their own efforts. Those efforts are possible because of the capacity they possess – whether individually or as a community. That capacity is part of what it means to be made in God's image.

In the world of service provision people become clients. Sometimes a person is a number or a statistic. When I go to see the doctor, I am actually handed a card with a number on it and I only enter the doctor's surgery when that number is called out. We have become so used to such client-provider relationships because they are the norm in our societal system.[12] The problem is that, when we take that mentality into working among the disadvantaged, the poor become impersonal. They become 'the poor' rather than individuals with names, contexts, histories, families and hopes for the future. Empowerment is a relational exchange. Empowerment can only take place through relationships and not through systems, however efficient those systems might be.

In his book on transformational development Bryant Myers talks about the importance of both identity and vocation. The poor need first of all to know that they are God's children and that they have inherent capacity to contribute to the wellbeing of the community. At the same time, those who aren't poor need to understand their identity in order to exercise their vocation in an empowering way.

While the agenda for the poor and the non-poor are the same, the issues of each are different. The poor suffer from a marred identity and a degraded vocation. The non-poor, on the other hand, suffer from god-complexes and an inflated vocation. The challenge to the poor is to recover their identity as children of God and to discover their vocation as productive stewards, discovering that they have been given gifts to contribute to social well-being. The challenge for the non-poor, including the development agency, is to relinquish their god-complexes and to employ their gifts for the sake of all human beings rather than using their gifts as a source of power or control.[13]

If the poor are going to be empowered to be productive stewards, those of us who are not poor are going to have to change. We are going to have to relinquish control and stop trying to be experts and teachers. Instead, we need to be facilitators and empowerers. That is a challenge for individuals and agencies who work among poor communities. It is also a challenge for governments, who rarely make investments in poor communities that don't come with strings attached.

The Incarnation as an Act of Empowerment

We have seen the principle of empowerment at work in the Old Testament, but it is there in the New Testament as well. In fact, the most striking example of empowerment is the incarnation. God became man. God did not send a message or a book or communicate in an impersonal way – he incarnated among us. God sending his son is the most incredible empowering act!

I have great respect for the organizations that have been birthed through the work of Viv Grigg, including Servant Partners and Servants to Asia's Urban Poor. These organizations are made up of individuals and families who choose to move into poor neighbourhoods around the world. In his book *The Urban Halo*, Craig Greenfield, who works with Servants to Asia's Urban Poor, tells the story of how he and his wife, Nay, moved into one of the slum communities in the city of Phnom Penh, the capital of Cambodia. It is a moving story of how their 'incarnating' among the poor led eventually to a wonderfully empowering programme of community-based care for orphans.[14] Whereas many would look upon orphans in a community as indicating deficiency and set up a home to care for them, Craig and Nay facilitated a programme that was built on the community's capacity to respond to their own needs.

Jesus' incarnation truly was an act of empowerment but, what is more, the way that Jesus lived reflected a God who seeks to empower. Jesus listened more than he talked. He gave people options rather than ultimatums. He asked as many questions as he gave answers. He acknowledged faith rather than demanded it. He prompted people to think for themselves rather than teaching dogmatic truth. He believed in the capacity of his disciples as he sent them out to do what he was doing. He believed in the capacity of the band of common people who followed him around as he said, 'You are the light of the world', 'You are the salt of the earth'. He never sought to control and always gave room for people to be themselves. Steve Chalke and Alan Mann make this point in their book, *The Lost Message of Jesus*:

> Too often we fail to look at others through the eyes of Jesus. While we have spent centuries arguing over the doctrine of original sin, poring over the Bible and huge theological tomes to prove the inherent sinfulness of all humankind, we have missed a startling point: Jesus believed in original

goodness! God declared that all his creation, including humankind, was very good.[15]

As I said in the introduction, this does not override our understanding of the sinfulness of all people but it accompanies that belief. In fact, it is where we should start with people – recognizing the amazing capacity that all people have (a belief that is theologically rooted in Genesis 1) prior to recognizing the sinfulness of all people (a belief that is rooted in Genesis 3).

As Jesus left the earth he gave his Holy Spirit to empower us so that we could be his hands and feet in the world. But note that the Holy Spirit does not force his way; he does not come to demand or control. He is patient and gentle and empowering, not overriding our will but working with us in the process of personal transformation. God is a God of empowerment and calls us to empower others. If we approach the poor seeing their capacity, and not their deficiency, and seeking to empower them to build a better world rather than trying to sort out their world for them, we might well be surprised by the outcome.

Because all people are made in the image of God, all people have inherent dignity. We respect the dignity of the poor as human beings who possess the same capacity that everyone else has. We therefore do not come to them thinking we know what they need and then give it to them. Rather, we come to them seeking to empower them to be in control of their own lives, choices and destiny.

7

Compassion

I see God in every human being. When I wash the leper's wounds, I feel I am nursing the Lord himself. Is it not a beautiful experience?

– Mother Teresa[1]

All people are made in the image of God, and his concern and compassion are for all. God does not love the poor any more than he loves those who have resources, friends, and opportunity, yet his compassion is exercised towards them because of the pain and suffering of their situations. God holds the pain of the world and invites us to share some of that with him. As we do, we will find ourselves among the poor and broken of our world as the hands and feet of Jesus. And, as we do that, we will find God's compassion for all he has made welling up within us.

When Sonia's parents were unable to make repayments on a loan they had taken out to buy her father's cycle-rickshaw, they asked her to get a job. She was eleven years old, and she reluctantly went off to work at a job cutting threads on sweaters and carrying them between factory floors. She was forced to work both day and night shifts for as long as 15 days, without being allowed to leave the fac-tory. She was beaten regularly for sitting down when she was tired.

Her health suffered. She earned about $15 a month. After two months her family agreed she could stop, and she returned to school. Our project staff noticed how much she had changed. Before she left she had been such a happy child. After medical attention, some support and encouragement, her smile star-ted to return. She said that there were about a hundred other young girls working in that factory.

Sonia lives in Duaripara, a slum community of approximately twelve thousand people in Dhaka, Bangladesh. Many of those who live there are young girls who miss out on schooling because their parents can't afford the school fees. So these girls are expected to look after younger siblings, collect water and help with cooking and cleaning. Once they reach their teenage years, the expectations change as they face pressure to supplement the family income by getting a job in one of the local garment factories. Regardless of what Western companies say about not selling products that have been manufactured through child labour, the truth is that a lot of children still work when they should be having a childhood. For the past four years Oasis has worked in that slum community in partnership with the Church of Bangladesh in a project that seeks to help the most vulnerable girls get into the schooling system and stay there once enrolled or, if this is not feasible, to help them access informal educational opportunities around other responsibilities. Our work has focused on the families, seeing these vulnerable girls in the context of their wider community.

Just recently, however, one of our staff members working in that project stood in front of the half-demolished slum where the girls live and wept. She wept because many of these teenage girls had just lost not only their homes and belongings but also a significant amount of their personal security. In the space of two hours, at the hands of those who should be there to protect the interests of those who are most vulnerable, their lives had been turned upside down. Government bulldozers had come to do so-called 'justice', but that simply meant protecting the rights of those with wealth, power, and influence who laid claim to the land at the expense of the poor who had lived there for years and also had legitimate rights. We can understand why she was weeping – it was just so unfair.

Sharing the Pain of God

The extent of need in our world must break God's heart. There is no point reciting the statistics of those without even the basics of food and clean water, opportunity or hope.[2] The statistics themselves have become meaningless because none of us can really imagine what a few million or billion looks like. The numbers are just too large to get our heads around. Though statistics are often used to motivate people to involvement, on many occasions they just tell us that the problem is beyond our capability to resolve. And most of us, when faced with such overwhelming odds, will wisely turn on some defence mechanism in order to hold on to our sanity. Statistics are great for shock value, but they do little else. They certainly do not instil compassion – that comes from another source. But these overwhelming needs in our world surely do break the heart of God. If it were not so we would have little hope, because hope comes from knowing that, although we cannot comprehend the pain and suffering and injustice in our world, God can and does. He holds it all.

Gary Haugen, who founded International Justice Mission following his experiences as part of the United

Nation's genocide investigations team in Rwanda in 1994, points out that 'at the root of God's compassion is the fact that he sees, witnesses, directly observes the suffering of the abused'.[3] Gary's journey of trying to come to terms with what he had witnessed in Rwanda led him to contemplate this in an unusual way.

> The thought led me to imagine what it must be like for God to be present, this year, at the rape of all the world's child prostitutes, at the beatings of all the world's prisoners of conscience, at the moment the last breath of hope expires from the breast of each of the millions of small children languishing in bonded servitude. As I would approach my God in prayer, I could hear his gentle voice saying to me, 'Son, do you have any idea where your Father has been lately?'[4]

As God holds the pain and suffering of the world, he invites us to share a small portion of it with him – not to take on more than we can bear, but to feel the pain of one person or one community. Perhaps it is the pain that Sonia faces or the pain of the Duaripara community where she lives. Perhaps it is the homeless person we walk past on our way to work or the group of teenage mothers who hang out in the park. Perhaps it is a group of street children or child soldiers or abused women. Perhaps it is the community we live in or one on the other side of the world. Not too much. Not the millions of children who live on the streets or the millions who go to bed hungry, just the ones and twos. This is God's invitation to us, to share the pain of his heart for a few of the broken, the despised, the poor. We don't have the capability or capacity to share God's pain for the whole world, but we do have enough for a few. This is not about taking on responsibility for something or someone. It is, first and foremost, about joining God in holding the pain of others. We don't take it from him. He doesn't hold the pain any less because we now share it. But we hold it with him and, as we do, we begin a journey of discovery and engagement. This is where compassion begins – compassion for others who like us have been made in God's image. It is built not on the statistics of suffering but on the knowledge that one person is of inestimable value because each and every human being has been made in God's image.

Being Overwhelmed

Sometimes when we get involved among the poor it is easy to forget this truth that God is holding the pain and suffering of our world. We get so involved in meeting people's needs, in setting up programmes and projects to ease the pain of others and to create opportunity, that our focus changes slightly. Instead of sharing the pain that God feels for a suffering world, we begin holding it ourselves, on our own. We begin to think that the welfare of others depends exclusively on us – that somehow we are the answer. When we do that, we are one small step away from becoming overwhelmed.

Jude Tiersma Watson has lived as part of an inner-city ministry in downtown Los Angeles for many years. As she reflected on the challenges of working among the broken and rejected in an urban environment she said this,

If we allow the desperate need of the city to be our starting point, it will not take long before we are completely overwhelmed. This is perhaps the key to how Mother Teresa has continued so many years in such difficult work. In a television interview several years ago she was asked, 'How did you receive your call to serve the poor?' Without missing a beat she replied, 'My call is not to serve the poor. My call is to follow Jesus. I have followed him to the poor. But if he called me to the rich, I would go to the rich.'[5]

It is easy to feel overwhelmed when the needs around us are so great. Everyone who has worked for any length of time among the poor has had that experience. In an instant we can feel so alone, so weak, so helpless. We want to make a difference but discover that our small offering is insignificant in the light of the needs we see. It is then that we need to return to an understanding of how God holds the pain of the world. Our role is to join him in sharing it. Without that perspective, we become overwhelmed – and that leads either to paralysis or burn-out.

Most people who work for any length of time among the urban poor will tell you of the times they have felt overwhelmed. It is a common experience. Yet it is also common to feel yourself becoming hardened. I remember an experience I had in 1996 when a group of visitors came to see our work in Mumbai. Many groups had visited us over the years, and we had worked out ways of letting them see what we were doing without interfering too much with the work. Deciding how much to show them was always difficult. On the one hand, we knew that some of the people among whom we were working might misunderstand the presence of these visitors. On the other hand, we had seen many people's hearts touched by what they witnessed among us and the changes in focus and priority that they made as a result once they returned home.

On this particular day I was taking a group of visitors downtown, in the early evening, to see some of the sights. As we walked along one of the more crowded parts of Grant Road, a group of children came up and grabbed hold of my legs. I stopped and asked them to let go, but they refused. Some others close by, who knew that this was a tactic they would use against unsuspecting tourists, also told them to let go. But they held on. After a few minutes of waiting I began to get a little anxious – first, because the folk I was taking round had gone on ahead and I didn't want to lose them; second, because here I was, the expert, showing people around, and I was the one in trouble. Eventually I managed to free my legs, only to have the same couple of kids grab hold of them again a few yards further down the road.

Nothing I said to them made any difference. They just held on for dear life, waiting for me to put my hand in my pocket and pull out some money. I felt taken advantage of in the extreme. You see, these were the kind of youngsters among whom I worked. They didn't know that, of course, but this is how they made their living and, not being respecters of persons, they were not going to let up just because I was able to string some Hindi together. Eventually I pulled myself free for the second time and managed to catch up with the others. As we continued down the road, though, I had this aching feeling in my stomach. Why had I reacted in that way to those children? I worked with children very like them in another part of the city. Yet in this context I was not meeting them on my terms, and my feelings of being taken advantage of and of anger against them produced a soul-searching in me that was to continue for some time. How could I be so hard-hearted? Why was I more concerned about losing sight of friends for a few minutes than I was about these children who probably had had no home for years? Why did I react in exactly the way that I had, on numerous occasions, suggested others should not react?

How could I forget the fact that each of these precious children had been made in God's image? Why could I not therefore share God's pain for them even for a moment?

In the city there are often beggars at the side of the road or on the steps leading up to the station. Many place bowls in front of them, others just sit or lie, and some walk around holding out the stub end of a hand or leg. There is a sense in which one almost grows used to this, though that is worrying in and of itself. On occasion we stopped and helped people. Sometimes it meant taking someone to a hospital, other times it meant buying the person a cup of tea or praying with them. One day I was walking over the footbridge at Bandra station and noticed a teenage boy lying on the ground with a bloodied leg. It looked awful. As I walked past him the gentle voice of the Holy Spirit urged me to stop, but I was in the process of gaining back my equilibrium, having just come off one of the packed commuter trains (they were so packed you could never even be sure whether you would make it off at your station or not). I was also in a rush to get to a meeting. Although I can't remember what the meeting was about, it was probably something to do with helping people in need, since that is what we did. I decided not to stop. As I walked on, though, what I had just done began to hit me. Here I was, working in a city with so much need but, instead of listening to the promptings of the Spirit, I walked straight by because I was late for a meeting about how to help people like the one I had just ignored. Again, my heart was in turmoil as I grappled with why I had reacted as I did. How could I do such a thing? Even more worrying to me was the fact that I was able to come up with a whole range of rational reasons in my own mind as to why I had done the right thing.

Becoming Hardened

It is sometimes the small incidents like this one that have a profound impact on our understanding of who we really are. The role they play in bringing us face to face with our own inadequacy is out of proportion to their seeming significance at the time.

These sometimes seemingly insignificant daily events have the power to show us our inadequacy to control or order what we think should happen. We end up being surprised not only by our own reactions, but also by how much they are motivated by pride and self-interest. We begin to ask a new set of questions. How can we ensure that our hearts do not become hardened like those of so many around us who seem oblivious to the needs of the poor? We condemn their attitudes, only to discover that we are in danger of exhibiting hardness of the same kind. How do we maintain compassion for the needy in the face of so much suffering, when our natural human instinct is to get used to it as a part of what life throws up but fails to answer? How do we allow ourselves to be vulnerable when we are supposed to be strong enough to help others? What happens when we encounter need that is aggressive and not on our terms?

Robert Lupton recounts a story in his beautiful little book *Theirs Is the Kingdom*. Early one morning he discovered that a homeless person had spent the night in his car. He reacted, as we would probably all have done, with a clenched fist. He documents his reaction almost immediately afterwards.

The Christ, the despised one, the one from whom we hid our faces, spoke softly, deeply in my spirit. It was the voice of one who himself claimed to have no place to lay his head. I began to weep. I remembered my clenched fist and my compassionless expulsion of this stranger from my life. I cried in sorrow for a broken man whom I had sent off into the cold – unshowered, unfed. And I sorrowed for one whose heart is not yet sufficiently broken, whose heart hardens too quickly against the call of the Lord among the least of these.

I am sorry Lord, for turning you out into the cold. Thank you for using my car.[6]

If being overwhelmed is a danger on one hand, then becoming hardened is a danger on the other. It is never pleasant to discover that my compassion is skin-deep. Such shallowness has often been revealed to me at times when the unexpected happens and I don't have time to measure my reaction or when someone takes advantage of me.

One afternoon a complete stranger phoned our office. It was not uncommon to receive such a call, but what was unusual was that this person said that someone in a bookshop near Victoria terminus had told him he should see me. I agreed to meet him that evening at home. It was a regular part of life to meet people with one kind of need or another so we could assess their situation. We had to decide whether we should get involved ourselves or refer them to someone else, or whether, on the suspicion that they might not be genuine, we should refuse help altogether.

When there was a knock at the door that evening, a reasonably well-spoken, yet quite poorly dressed, young man walked in. He first told me about how he had been put in touch with me and what he wanted. It seemed quite genuine. He was an accountant by profession, he said, and he had married a girl from north-east India and had moved there with her. But, since his family were Hindu, when he married this girl from a Christian home his family wanted nothing to do with him. While he was in the North-East something had gone wrong, his new wife left him, and he began a drug habit that eventually led to him being arrested and put into prison. There he continued to inject himself when he could lay his hands on some heroin. At one point he lifted up his shirt to show us the old scars all over his body – from both his drug use and the beatings he had received while in the jail. He told us that some missionaries visited the prison and that their impact left him with a deep desire to follow God and to reform his life. When he was released he had enough money to return to Mumbai, but his parents were still in no mind to help him and he was out on the streets. His plan was to return to north-east India by train and, now that he had his degree certificates in hand, he hoped to find another job there. He was also keen to find his wife and, if at all possible, to repair their marriage.

It was an incredible story and, as Joan and I listened to him, we felt we were listening to another testimony of God's grace in a person's life. His use of spiritual language spoke of a personal and intimate walk with the Lord. After a couple of hours of discussion and having fed him an evening meal, we gave him 2,000 rupees (about $50) for the train that would leave the following morning at five o'clock. Before he left we prayed for him, and he also thanked the Lord for his goodness and grace in his life. It was moving to hear him pray. We reminded him to keep in touch and to let us know how he got on.

About a week to ten days later, Dave, who headed up a project among some of the older street boys, phoned for advice. He'd received a phone call from a young man who needed help. They had talked quite extensively on the phone and Dave had ascertained that he had just arrived from north-east India and was keen to return to be with his wife. As we talked, that horrible familiar feeling came over me. I had been duped once again.

It's so easy to put up our defences against being taken for a ride – to give to nobody to make sure we don't get ripped off, to decide that we will be the arbiter of what is genuine need and what is not. The problem is that when we do that our hearts begin to close, ever so subtly, towards the poor. The soft ground in which compassion grows turns to sun-baked soil in which it is hard to grow anything. I remember hearing Jackie Pullinger once say, 'Whatever you do, whether you give to a person or not, don't close your heart to the poor.'[7] That is something I have tried to put into practice – though I have not always been successful. It is not easy to be the compassionate hands and feet of Jesus among the poor without becoming either hardened or overwhelmed. We need God's help.

The Way of Jesus

Scripture shows us that Jesus extended compassion at different levels. Most often we see his compassion for people he met – including the man with leprosy,[8] the widow at Nain[9] whose only son had just died, and many others. In a lovely incident at Bethsaida,[10] a group of people brought a blind friend to Jesus and begged him to touch him. Jesus chose not simply to touch him but to take his hand and lead him out of the city before healing him. I like to imagine what it must have been like walking hand in hand with Jesus! Then there was the expression of compassion Jesus had for people generally, for the crowds and multitudes who followed him and who were 'harassed and helpless, like sheep without a shepherd'.[11] It was this compassion that led Jesus to provide food for large crowds on two occasions.[12] Jesus also expressed compassion towards the whole city of Jerusalem. Luke 13:34 records Jesus' words, 'O Jerusalem, Jerusalem, you who kill the prophets and stone those sent to you, how often I have longed to gather your children together, as a hen gathers her chicks under her wings, but you were not willing!'[13] Luke later records how, as Jesus entered Jerusalem just prior to his death and resurrection, he wept for the city.[14]

Some scholars have noted that Jesus neither healed all those he saw nor met every need he encountered, and yet Jesus never became hardened or overwhelmed. What was it about him that enabled him to sustain such compassion amidst the needs of his time? To answer this question we need to look at the broader picture that Scripture presents.

A wider framework

Scripture shows us that Jesus operated with a wider perspective. He wasn't simply seeking to meet people's needs. He had a growing realization of who he was and what he was called to accomplish, and he saw engaging with people in need within that framework. He often articulated his desire to do his Father's will[15] and, as part of that, he engaged in relieving the suffering of those around him. Jesus both articulated and demonstrated that his presence at that particular point in history was ushering in the kingdom of God – fullness of life, in every area, to all people. Dewi Hughes, in his book *God of the Poor*, suggests that the 'kingdom of God' should also be the framework for those of us who work among the poor.

> Christians working among the poor, therefore need to keep their vision strongly on the ultimate goal for humanity which is the Kingdom of God.[16]

This is the view of many others as well, including Malcolm Duncan, who until recently led the Faithworks movement that was birthed out of Oasis and remains a key part of the Oasis strategy. He writes,

> The fundamental purpose of the Christian church, and therefore of every local congregation, is to realise God's kingdom. It is the kingdom of God that lies at the heart of the teaching, life and action of the Lord Jesus and it is this kingdom that pervades His parables, His miracles, and His passion.[17]

Having a 'kingdom' perspective as we work among the poor is about seeing their needs and the injustice they face within the wider spiritual, social and political context. It is about seeing the present in the context of the future. It is about seeing poverty in the context of having life 'to the full'.[18]

Miracle

It is interesting that when Jesus shows compassion for people this is often accompanied by a demonstration of the kingdom of God breaking into a person's life in a miraculous way. The leper was healed, the son of the widow of Nain was raised from the dead, and when Jesus had compassion on the crowds they all had plenty to eat with plenty left over.

Without the miraculous intervention of God in the lives of those amongst whom we work it would be difficult, if not impossible, to sustain hope. The intervention of God into situations of seeming hopelessness is one of the greatest sustaining factors for those who work among the poor. Of course we would love to see miracles on demand, but that is not God's way. We have no answers for why, on many occasions, our prayers for God's miraculous intervention in a person's life seem to go unheard. Yet that occasional breakthrough, as people are healed or delivered or witness God's kingdom break through in another way, is vital in sustaining us in the midst of the pain and suffering of those around us.

Flexibility and focus

Jesus never seems to have been caught out by the unexpected, even though it was a regular occurrence in his life. On several occasions his plans appeared to change because of the invitation or need of others, yet he remained unfazed. As we saw in Chapter 3, in Mark 5, when Jesus arrived on the other side of Galilee he was approached by Jairus, a synagogue ruler whose daughter was dying. Jesus went with him, but then he was touched by a woman who had suffered with a serious medical condition for 12 years. Jesus spent time in conversation with this woman only to then be told that it was too late to go to Jairus' home, because his daughter had already died. Jesus simply carried on with his original plan and raised the girl from the dead. No need seemed so pressing that he was rushed; no need seemed so insignificant that it could be ignored. Jesus was not wandering around aimlessly, yet he was not so fixed to a tight agenda that he had no room for flexibility. He was somehow both focused and flexible and, because of that, he was neither overwhelmed by the needs he met nor distracted by the ones he didn't.

When structures and schedules are too tight, we lose valuable opportunities to respond to the voice of God when the unexpected happens. If in our projects and programmes we operate a personal schedule that leaves no time for the unexpected and we have a mindset that is fixed on specific goals, there will be little room for manoeuvre. Somehow, in the midst of our structures and timetables, we must keep our focus while also maintaining flexibility.

Sometimes, too, we need to dig a bit deeper to examine our reasons and motivations for establishing programmes. It is possible that in creating them we are actually shielding ourselves from the pain of those we serve. They can become a defence mechanism that gives us meaning because we feel like we are doing something when in fact what is really needed is just an expression of empathy – of being with another in the midst of their pain. As Mary Thiesen reflects on her experience,

> In this environment of physical, spiritual, mental, and emotional onslaughts, it is almost inevitable to respond to disorder by creating order, to crisis by taking action, to neediness by providing resources, to problems by seeking solutions, and to chaos by imposing control. The conscious and subconscious tendency is to establish rules to ensure safety, to define doctrine to preserve purity, to set up programs to enhance productivity, to insist on schedules and reports to guarantee success, to build buildings to offer visible proof of change, to outline procedures to prevent failure, and to devise policies to prevent uncertainty and insecurity.[19]

As I reflect on this, I can see myself striving to demonstrate visible proof of change in those I seek to help. I find it so difficult to simply 'be' with the poor, yet it seems the easiest thing in the world to design another programme which I think will make a difference. I still have a long way to go. Real compassion does not jump to solutions immediately but allows time for true identification with the poor and requires a willingness to enter into their pain so as to understand them, and their situation, more fully. What the poor need and desire are people who are willing and able to understand, at least in some measure, the powerlessness of their situation. When you sit and talk with a beggar or visit a family in the slums, you have done everything that they could want: you have treated them with dignity and respect; you have come alongside them as a fellow human being in the struggles of life; you have ministered to their need for friendship and purpose. When you throw food or clothes or even services at them, you communicate that you want to control, to make a difference, to sort out their situation rather than having to enter into their powerlessness.

Compassion Is Not Enough

It is absolutely crucial for those who work among the poor to have, and to continue to develop, true compassion. But compassion exercised without wisdom can actually end up harming those we seek to serve. Many well-meaning people, out of a heart of compassion, seek to serve the poor but end up instead doing things that totally go against the wisdom of practitioners who have years of experience. I know this because I have been there myself and made that mistake and I see others const-antly temp-ted to do so. I don't know how many times people have asked me for advice about setting up an orphanage for kids – but in virtually all situations an orphanage is the last option that should be considered. Compassion needs to be supplemented by wisdom. We should always aim to be God-inspired, God-led, and God-reliant – and also totally professional. Getting the right balance between our focus on God and our professionalism is a constant challenge, but they need not be mutually exclusive.

Wisdom will always seek the best solution for those we want to help, and often the best solution is not the quickest or even the seemingly most compassionate alternative. Giving to meet immediate need may, over time, preclude an empowering response that helps people do something about their own situation. It may take time for people to catch the vision for change in their community, but this is absolutely essential if long-term sustainable transformation is to occur.

All people are made in the image of God, and his concern and compassion are for all. God does not love the poor any more than he loves those who have resources, friends, and opportunity, yet his compassion is exercised towards them because of the pain and suffering of their situations. God holds the pain of the world and invites us to share some of that with him. As we do, we will find ourselves among the poor and broken of our world as the hands and feet of Jesus. And, as we do that, we will find God's compassion for all he has made welling up within us.

8

Justice

Our standing in solidarity with the single parent, the unemployed, the refugee, our joining the God of the oppressed to work for justice in the world, doesn't just make a difference for those who are suffering. It rescues us.

– Rob Bell[1]

One day I received a phone call from Vijay, one of the boys we were working amongst on Kandivili station in Mumbai. He told me that three of the boys who lived on the side of the railway tracks there had been arrested by the police. He asked if I could come down and help sort it out. What he told me indicated that this was more serious than the usual kind of incident in which the police would pick up a boy sleeping around the station and put him away for a night or two – at festival times,

Because all people are made in the image of God, we need to treat them all equally. A key principle which undergirds any judicial system is equity. Injustice occurs when people are treated differently from one another. When a society is unjust it is always the poor who suffer most. If we are going to see the image of God restored among the poor, we are going to have to engage in issues of justice.

for example, when the police had to show they were in control by producing statistics recording how many 'anti-social' elements they had arrested. What used to alarm me in those early days was not so much the fact that this happened but rather the way in which the street children simply accepted it as part of life. But when Vijay explained that a railway carriage had been burnt down ten days previously and the police had just arrested around sixty people who they thought might have had something to do with it, including these three boys, a colleague and I went down to the station.

Vijay's concern was that, the longer the boys were held, the more likely it was that they would be forced to sign a confession. And he knew that they were innocent of the crime. Vijay was a key leader of this group and someone we had grown to trust. As cases can take years to go to trial, the boys would probably remain in prison for a considerable amount of time and, once they were sent down to the main jail, there would be little chance either for them to get out or for people to get in to see them. We had to act quickly, so we went to the court and talked it through with a lawyer. He told us that, in order to be considered for bail by the judge, the boys would need to get signed affidavits from three people who could all produce a series of documents including ration cards, income-tax returns and many other papers – none of which, of course, anyone in that community would have. As we were talking, a man came up to us and said that he could supply three people to undertake that on their behalf, but that he would charge a fee. I could hardly believe it, but he was a broker who did this for a living. We arranged to meet him again the following day.

The next day the broker was nowhere to be found, so we asked the lawyer whether there was any other way of obtaining a bail injunction. He said that he would be happy to file a representation with the judge for each of them to be bailed for the amount of 2,000 rupees each – a quite substantial figure. I went back to our staff team to discuss this, and in the end we all pitched in and collected that amount. The lawyer then filed a petition that was accepted by the judge and the three were discharged.

Over the subsequent years we kept abreast of developments and, three and a half years later, the case finally came to court. All three boys were acquitted of the crime, along with many others, because there had been no evidence in the first place. I then tried to recoup the bail money and spent a further 600 rupees and quite some effort, but without success. I'm not sure how many of the original sixty people remained in jail for those three and half years and then were acquitted, but the three we knew were definitely the fortunate ones. The incident demonstrated the injustice and corruption of a system that was biased against the poor. When corruption permeates a society it is the poor who suffer, not the rich.

Throughout the years we spent in Mumbai our lives were taken up with incidents like this one. We sought to help individuals and communities in their struggle to survive a system that was pitted against them. Our staff members spent a lot of time at hospitals, prisons and police stations, standing with prostitutes, street children and people from the slums, being a voice for those who needed the voice of another to speak for them. It was not that these people did not have voices of their own, it was simply that those in power would not listen to them.

Involvement with the Poor Means Involvement in Issues of Justice

You cannot get involved among the poor and not get involved in issues of justice. I think it is true the other way round, too – if you get involved in issues of justice you will end up engaging with the poor. Injustices, of course, can and do happen to people from all socio-economic backgrounds, but those of us who are from middle-class or wealthy backgrounds generally know we have recourse to address injustices when they occur. Our education enables us to articulate the injustice that has occurred and to seek to put it right, whether personally or through the judicial system. The poor cannot do this. If you are poor and suffer an injustice, where are you going to get the money to hire a lawyer to plead your case in court when you don't even have money to feed your family?

The judicial system favours those who have resources over those without them. And when, as in some parts of the world, the system of justice is itself corrupt, it becomes weighted even more heavily against the poor. Corruption is rife, and those with resources simply use them to pay their way through to obtain judgements in their favour. In this world, money truly is power.

In the Western world, one of the results of making the gospel into simply an issue of personal salvation is that people have been able to ignore issues of justice because they are primarily about what happens in community and between people. Only recently has the evangelical church in the West begun to wake up to the all-encompassing nature of God's engagement with the world and the fact that the good news has implications for all of life. Mark Labberton challenges us to reconnect our worship with a life of justice.

The life-changing good news of God's saving love in Jesus Christ encompasses every dimension of our humanity and every aspect of God's re-creation of the world. Evangelism explains and calls people to respond to Jesus

In His Image

Christ, who wants to make every person and everything (including every form of injustice and oppression) new. That is our hope and our commission as God's people. This holistic vision is the heart of God for the world. Our theology and our worship are meant to reflect that through lives that share God's heart for righteousness and justice.[2]

Labberton further emphasizes that the two great commandments cannot be separated – to love God and to love our neighbour. When they are separated they can both become distorted. Our worship of God can become self-seeking and our hearts can be hardened to the needs of our neighbour. Labberton urges us to take note of the Old Testament prophets, who clearly articulate the dualistic nature of Israel's communal life. How was it, we ask, that they could worship, fast, pray, and continue all of their usual 'spiritual' routines, yet oppress their neighbour? Yes, it wasn't just that they ignored the plight of the poor – it was that they oppressed them.[3]

For all our apparent passion about God, in the end much of our worship seems to be mostly about us. We presume we can worship in a way that will find God but lose track of our neighbor. Yet it was this very pattern in Israel's worship life that brought God's judgment. Biblical worship that finds God will also find our neighbor.[4]

This perspective is shared by many others, including Steve Chalke and Simon Johnston, who make the same point when they say that true spirituality is a combination of both intimacy with God and engagement in society. This, again, reflects the belief that the two great commandments cannot be separated from each other.[5]

Living Righteously

I grew up with an understanding that to live righteously was to do with an absence of certain things in my life. I had the idea that, if I avoided a whole bunch of things that were off-limits for someone seeking to follow God's ways, then I would be deemed to be living righteously. In fact, the picture I had was of myself spending a whole day in my room lying on my bed not thinking, not speaking – not doing anything. If I could do that for a 24-hour period, then at least I could be deemed to have followed God's command to live righteously for a day. Many people have this view of righteousness – an absence of sin in a person's life. Yet this is not biblical. True righteous living is not simply about what we avoid; it is also about what we actively do. Time and again Scripture urges us to help the weak, the poor, the helpless and the marginalized. Living righteously is active. One of the reasons that books like Leviticus are in the Bible is that they give us an idea of what a righteous community, where people relate to each other in a godly way, would look like.

At the heart of the book of Leviticus is the principle of Jubilee[6] that we discussed in Chapter 2. If any community, at any time, implemented Jubilee, they would witness a more radical outworking of equity than has ever been seen. The principle is about creating a system that gives a time-bound limit on the effects of poverty on individuals within a community. It provided a fresh start for those Israelites who had not done so well in the previous time-bound period. If you had to sell your property, or you got into debt, or you became a slave, all that changed in the fiftieth year. Jubilee ensured a restoration of the means of creating wealth and therefore of opportunity. It protected the most vulnerable and gave them another chance to prosper. Of course, God could demand this of the people of Israel because the land was his, not theirs. It stemmed from that one key understanding – that the people were *all* tenants.[7]

There is no indication that the people of Israel ever practised Jubilee in a widespread way. In fact, there is evidence that over time they completely lost the understanding of God's ownership of the land – this in turn led not only to permanent poverty for some, but also to the oppression of the poor by the rich. Just imagine what could happen if the church today were to regain the understanding that we are all tenants and that God is the owner. We would hold possessions more loosely; we would seek after a much more equitable distribution of wealth; we would work out ways of ensuring that people in our communities who became poor could start afresh. I think it would have a profound impact on our world.

When Systems of Justice are Unjust the Poor Suffer Most

In many parts of the world, one of the most disturbing things about injustice is that the very mechanism that is supposed to ensure justice for all becomes the tool of injustice among the poor. One day when my wife Joan was on her way to the school that our children attended in Mumbai she noticed a crowd of men gathered near the school gate. When she got closer she could see that the centre of attention was a policeman, both of whose hands were wrapped around a man's head as he banged it against the metal frame of his tea-stall. She realized that this man risked being seriously injured so she decided to intervene. She went over to the policeman and respectfully asked him to stop. Perhaps it was the shock of a white lady speaking Hindi that got his attention, but fortunately for the tea-stall owner he did stop. After apologizing to Joan, the policeman gathered himself and walked away.

The tea-stall owner was clearly grateful and set about trying to gather his belongings that the policeman, in his rage, had disbursed. Like thousands of others, he was a man seeking to make a living and feed his family. While it could be true that the tea-stall owner had been breaking the law in operating without a licence, there is a right way to deal with that under the law. When those operating on behalf of the law take matters into their own hands, injustice is always the outcome. Worse still, when the rule of law is corrupted and a person lives off the informal payments of those breaking the law, then injustice will only lead to further injustice – it becomes systemic, a way of life.

It is no surprise, then, that some people believe that the absence of justice is the primary cause of poverty.

We submit that the biblical evidence and the present situation point to the lack of justice as the principal – and practically exclusive – cause of poverty. This does not mean that we wish to minimize the complexity of the different realities of poverty in the world today, but we do wish to propose, together with the prophets of ancient Israel, that injustice generates contexts of poverty.[8]

Injustice Is Both Personal and Systemic

There is a difference between the specific injustices that the poor face and the system of injustice that traps people in their poverty. In other words, personal and systemic injustice are not the same thing. When a child is forced to work for 15 hours a day in dangerous conditions and is not paid because his parents sold him into that situation of bonded labour, he suffers a personal injustice. When that child's labour is the manufacture of clothing which is exported to another country and sold for twenty times the cost of the labour and materials, it becomes clear that his predicament is as much to do with trade policy, government agreements and the use of power as it is to do with specific individuals. Those who are poor are often the victims of both personal and systemic injustice.

And injustice is prevalent in communities around the world – even those that believe that following a democratic process should preclude them from injustice. At the church we run in Waterloo, London, Pete Brierley, who used to head up our youth work there, was constantly required to advocate for members of the youth group simply because of their colour. Duke and Melvin, aged sixteen and seventeen respectively, are two young people beginning to develop a passion for God as they stand in opposition to an unfair prejudice against black youths of their age. As they left the church one Sunday morning, they had barely walked twenty feet when they were stopped by four policemen. There had just been a mugging in the area by 'two black youths in hoodies'. Duke and Melvin tried to explain that they had been in church, but the police laughed at their pleas and treated them roughly and with little respect. It was only when Pete and a few other white folk with him were able to advocate on their behalf and assure the police that they had in fact been in the church service that they were allowed to go. There was no apology, just a strong rebuke: 'Don't look guilty in the future.' If being black means looking guilty, then they were guilty as charged – but surely the colour of their skin cannot be reason enough to treat them as they were treated. There are a disproportionate number of black young people treated as criminals simply because they are with friends and wearing hoodies. The UK Home Office statistics for 2007–08 showed that black youths were almost eight times more likely to be stopped than white youths.

Research carried out by Mori in 2004 showed that young people as a group are misrepresented and misunderstood. Seventy-one percent of the articles in newspapers about young people are negative. One in three articles about young people relates to crime. Only 8% of articles about young people actually quote young people. Injustice is both personal and systemic.

When we work among the disadvantaged we will frequently encounter personal injustice. Our role is that of an advocate – to stand with them as they seek to be dealt with on an equitable basis. Sometimes we discover that those who have been broken too easily accept injustice and choose not to respond. They become accepting of the way things are, never thinking that this is not how God intended things to be. Sometimes those who are poor accept injustice as if God had sanctioned it. They accept that, because of birth circumstances, others have a right to trample on them without conscience. Well, this is our message for them,

> God hates injustice! He won't stand for bribery and corruption that keep you alienated. He doesn't condone the oppression you face at the hands of those in power. God is on your side! Shouting above the storm – speaking out about injustice, standing up for the poor, taking a stand on justice issues – is preaching the gospel. It is our mission because it is Jesus' mission, which is God's mission.[9]

God Suffered Injustice

What a powerful thing it is to see someone who has suffered injustice have the eyes of their heart opened as they come to realize that God also suffered injustice at the hands of the powerful. He, too, was alienated and persecuted and paid the ultimate cost – his life. God understands how it feels to be a victim of both personal and systemic injustice. What is more, Jesus suffered injustice at the hands of the powerful and influential primarily because they could not accept what he stood for – justice! He came to release the oppressed, free the prisoners, bring sight to the blind. His message was one of inclusion, that everybody has a place in the good purposes of God, that all are equal, all are made in his image, all can receive the fullness of life he came to bring. The religious leaders didn't have him crucified just because Jesus claimed to be God. They had him crucified because, while he claimed to be God, he didn't fit into their picture of what God was like. Instead he preached good news to the poor, sat with the outcasts, and welcomed those who were 'sinners'. At one level it is true to say that Jesus was crucified because he wasn't the Messiah the religious leaders were expecting. Instead, he stood for justice in an unjust world. What an amazing truth for someone facing injustice to understand.

At the end of his famous mandate speech in the synagogue in Nazareth Jesus referred to the Jubilee – the day of the Lord's favour. This was the day when everyone would stand on a level playing field, when those who had faced misfortune could start afresh all over again, when justice reigned supreme because the system was reborn. There has been debate over whether this quotation from Isaiah 61 is to be read primarily as having spiritual connotations. Paul Hertig points out that a true reading integrates both social and spiritual dimensions and gives equal balance to both action and proclamation. He goes on to say, 'Luke will not allow us to interpret this jubilee language as flowery metaphors or spiritual allegories.'[10]

So every time you stand with someone who is oppressed, someone who is a victim of the system, someone who has been alienated from the decision-making processes of life or someone who has been abused, you represent Jesus, who comes to breathe justice into our world. This is righteousness – not the absence of vices in your life, but standing with the oppressed seeking justice on their behalf.

Around the world, on a daily basis, our staff members come face to face with the injustices which those we serve suffer. The vast majority of these arise simply because of poverty. I think, for instance, of what happened to Kate, a beautiful fifteen-year-old girl from northern Uganda. Her aunt had convinced her parents that it would be good if she took her from their village and into the city to be educated. Sadly, though, she was never enrolled in a school and instead ended up working as a housemaid for a university lecturer and his family. The lecturer's wife was often out of town because of her work and, when their two young sons were asleep, the lecturer attempted on several occasions to get her to sleep with him. Kate was afraid to confront the lecturer or to tell his wife and did not want to break the family up. But Kate was attending the informal education programme run by Oasis, and she confided in one of the staff about her predicament. Our staff were obviously concerned for her safety, so they suggested that she stay at the Oasis halfway home. They then got in touch with the lecturer's wife to explain the situation. In the end the lecturer agreed to meet with Kate, together with his wife, in the presence of the Oasis staff. Even though he continued to deny what he had done, all those present could see that Kate was telling the truth. Kate is now enrolled in mainstream school and is doing well.

Jesus, of course, stood firmly opposed to the systemic injustice that was prevalent in his day. This was a key component of his discussions with the religious leaders. 'Woe to you, teachers of the law and Pharisees, you hypocrites! You give a tenth of your spices – mint, dill and cummin. But you have neglected the more important matters of the law – justice, mercy and faithfulness. You should have practised the latter, without neglecting the former.'[11] We never find Jesus speaking in such a way to one specific person, but there is no questioning the forceful way he addresses the religious leaders as a group. Systemic injustice is the result when groups of people or sections of society begin to operate out of a paradigm that views people as unequal. The fact that all people are made in God's image is a foundational truth for an equitable society. When people ignore that truth, the result is always injustice.

Equality and Equity

One of the fundamental reasons why injustice is perpetuated is because there is an alternative view of humankind in our world. In place of the wonderful truth that every single person is made in God's image and therefore of equal value, many people believe that some are more valuable than others. They believe that the family you are born into, your social standing, your occupation or qualifications or a host of other factors determine your value. This is not an issue only in countries that have a worldview shaped by non-Christian traditions. It is the reality in the West, too. After all, only within the last fifty years in both the USA and South Africa have blacks been given the same legal standing as whites. People everywhere have forgotten the fundamental truth that, because all people are made in the image of God, all people are therefore equal. And because all people are equal, the systems we create must be based on the foundation of equity.

As we stand with individuals who are poor and act as advocates on their behalf, seeking justice from oppression, we do God's work. And, when we do, people will see the hands and feet of Jesus.[12] The more we do this, the more we realize that systemic injustice has to be addressed – and that is best done not only on an individual basis but collectively as well. When people come together to advocate on behalf of whole groups of people, the impact they can have is so much greater. When each individual voice is added to thousands of others, those in authority cannot ignore us forever. We will look at the issue of collective advocacy in more depth in Chapter 12.

> Because all people are made in the image of God, we need to treat them all equally. A key principle which undergirds any judicial system is equity. Injustice occurs when people are treated differently from one another. When a society is unjust it is always the poor who suffer most. If we are going to see the image of God restored among the poor, we are going to have to engage in issues of justice.

9

Prayer

If all we are is strong, there is no hope for us. If all we need
is ourselves, there is no hope for the world.

– Danielle Speakman[1]

It was around nine o'clock in the morning on Tuesday, 30
January, when Sushila (whom we met in Chapter 2)
knocked on our front door. She collapsed on the floor as
I opened the door. Pain was written all over her face. I
helped her up and we made her some tea. Sushila began
to tell us about the severe pain she was experiencing in
her back and her legs. She could not sit or stand. She also
shared the deep concern she had for her youngest
daughter, Supna, who had been unwell for some time
and probably had measles. Life was hard for Sushila, as
it is for so many people who live without the kind of
safety nets that others of us
have for our health as well
as for other areas of our
lives.

> Because all people are made in the image of God, his ears are attentive to the cries of all people. When those who are poor cry out to him, he hears. When others cry out to him on their behalf, he hears.

We suggested to Sushila
that we pray with her,
something we had done on
a number of occasions

before. Joan sat next to her and placed her hands on her back as we prayed for that part of her body. We also spent time just quietly praying, not always filling the time with words, asking God to reveal himself to her. During the course of our prayer time it was obvious, from Sushila's groaning and movements as well as her oblivion to the surroundings, that the Holy Spirit was at work. When Sushila finally opened her eyes, she began to tell us what had happened while we were praying. In a vision she recognized herself as a young girl and had walked a long, long way out of the city and had come to a large building like a church. Inside she saw a man who looked like a priest whom she recognized as Jesus. He had spoken to her and told her to come forward. She went forward and knelt, but Jesus had taken hold of her hands and lifted her up and told her that she needn't cry anymore because she was going to be all right and her daughter was going to be all right too.

As Sushila recounted this vision to us her face lit up. We saw the burden of her own health and that of her daughter's being lifted from her. Joan and I felt as though we were on holy ground. We spent some more time in prayer, and then Joan accompanied her back to the slum to pray with Supna. On the way back Sushila was bounding and leaping along as she showed Joan the places where she had collapsed while on the way to our home a couple of hours earlier. She was anticipating her neighbours' amazement when they saw her walking so well. At Sushila's home Joan prayed with Supna, trusting that Jesus' words in the vision would be fulfilled and that she, too, would get well. Over the weeks that followed crises continued to come Sushila's way, but on each occasion she prayed and testified to a measure of peace in her life – as well as to some specific circumstantial changes.

One of those changes was the favour her husband received when the electricity company overcharged them. They contested the amount and the bill was reduced. Sushila had another ongoing concern – her husband's employment. The fact that he hadn't worked for many years placed the biggest burden on Sushila, whose income had to support the whole family. Amazingly, however, for some unknown reason around this time he began to have a growing desire to work. Sushila, of course, knew that God was answering her prayers. In fact, having been unwilling to do most things, he suddenly became willing to do almost anything. Eventually he became set on the idea of setting up a stall to sell lime juice. Sushila wasn't so keen on the idea since it involved paying bribes to the police in the area where he would work, in addition to some capital outlay. They didn't have that kind of money and the stall would not guarantee a stable income. We all continued to pray and, eventually, her husband changed his mind. He then heard about a watchman's job that was available in Chembur, some distance away. Again, Sushila was not keen on this prospect because the cost of travel would significantly eat into the small salary he would receive each month. The night before he had to accept or reject the job Sushila had a dream in which Jesus spoke to her, telling her that her husband should accept the job and God would see that he always had enough money to get to work. The next morning Sushila's husband was surprised when she recounted her dream and told him that he should accept the job. Throughout that first month her husband did indeed have the money to travel each day, apart from one Sunday when he only had enough money for the bus fare and not for the segment he would need to do by train. She prayed that he wouldn't get caught without a ticket, and he didn't. After a few weeks he was offered alternative employment, with a higher salary, that involved less complex travel arrangements. It is often not so much the change in circumstances we crave when we pray as much as it is the knowledge that God is with us in them. This was Sushila's experience.

On one occasion Joan was talking with Sushila about heaven and injustice, helping her to understand the Bible, and soon afterwards Sushila had a dream in which God confirmed all that Joan had said. In the dream God told her of a time and place where injustice will no longer be the norm, where crying will have disappeared, where there will no longer be any unhappiness. Here was an illiterate woman who could not read the Bible but who began to understand that God was on her side, that God looked down on her and wept alongside her, that God was preparing a place for her and that one day she would join him there.

God Is Already at Work

When we began working among the disadvantaged, my framework of thinking involved somehow taking God to people. I didn't realize that God was already at work and that I needed to join in with what he was already doing. Over the years I slowly began to see how God was already at work in the lives of those we encountered and in their communities. This was a powerful shift in my thinking.

Clare Nonhebel and a friend, Alan, began visiting homeless people living in London in the 1990s. In her book *Far from Home* she records the stories of individuals they got to know over a period of time and the variety of reasons why each ended up as 'homeless'. One of the things she discovered early on as well was that God was at work in many different ways in the lives of those she met.

> We were finding it a humbling experience, meeting people whose only home was the streets. They certainly had courage and perseverance beyond any we had ourselves. We had a strong suspicion they might already be closer to Jesus Christ in spirit than we were, with our relatively comfortable lives.[2]

Because all people are made in the image of God, God is continually at work in some way in the lives of all people. God's revelation of himself and his love might be as generic as the revelation through nature that Paul mentions in the book of Romans,[3] or it might be specific revelation through dreams and visions. It might be, as Don Richardson discovered while working among the Sawi tribes of New Guinea, a redemptive analogy placed at the heart of a community or culture.[4] Regardless of the manner in which he chooses to reveal himself, God is always working in the lives of people everywhere – in ways far beyond human imagining. As Bryant Myers reminds us,

> Helping people recover their true identity and vocation also requires that they learn to reread their history. God did not come into the life of the community with the arrival of the missionaries and certainly not with the arrival of the development agency. God has been active in the story of the community since the beginning of time.[5]

When our family arrived in Mumbai we had an experience that taught us that God was already ahead of us. God quickly reminded us that he was already there, that we did not 'bring him with us'. We needed to find a place to live, and because at the time the law of the land favoured tenants, many landlords were not eager to let out properties – even when they were vacant. John, who had worked with us in Mumbai from the beginning, was already in Mumbai and was looking out for possibilities for us. But when I arrived in advance of the family to see the available options, there was only one. A friend had asked my wife Joan what she should pray for us regarding the move, and she suggested people pray that we would find a ground-floor flat near a play area for the children. Although I was a bit discouraged that John had found only one place for me to look at, we arrived at this one place to find that it was a ground-floor flat right next to a play area. If you threw a stone from the steps of our flat, you could hit the swings. It was an incredible lesson reminding us that God was already there and had already prepared a place for us. We were simply joining him. I sometimes tell people that if I had known God was going to answer that prayer so specifically I would have added 'next to a golf course' too!

A few years later I was speaking at the commissioning service for Jo Hayles, who was moving to work with Oasis in Dhaka, Bangladesh. When I shared this story she decided to ask people to pray for several specific things in preparation for her search for a flat. When she got to Dhaka, the second flat she looked at fitted exactly what she and others had prayed for. When she chatted with the landlord she discovered that he was a former student of mine from a school I had taught at twenty years previously in North India. In Dhaka, a city of over ten million people, I knew no more than twenty. She was bowled over by this further confirmation that God was already there and at work. God's concern for these details only added to her excitement about joining him in what he was already doing.

In Acts 10 Peter found himself in a situation he had never been in before as he entered and ate in the home of a non-Jew. This might not seem radical to us, but for a first-century Jew it was radical indeed. And Peter never would have done this had it not been for a vision from God. What he did was so unusual that, after the event, the other leaders of the early church called him to Jerusalem to explain what he had done. But when Peter arrived at the home of Cornelius in Caesarea he discovered that God was already there, already at work, already involved in their lives. For Peter this was revolutionary – for despite the years he had spent with Jesus, still he had not grasped the fact that the 'good news' was for everyone. Only in Cornelius' home did this truth finally dawn on him. He said, 'I now realise how true it is that God does not show favouritism but accepts those from every nation who fear him and do what is right.'[6]

Encountering God before Understanding Him

When we began working among the disadvantaged I imagined that we would do a lot of teaching and preaching – a lot of telling people 'the gospel'. I soon came to realize that the starting point of faith among the poor is not an intellectual grasp of truth but an encounter with the living God. This was what made the difference for Sushila. It wasn't that she understood God and so began to pray. Rather, her desperation led her to pray, and through that God met with her on countless occasions. Faith came through encounter with the truth, not through hearing about the truth. Her understanding, of course, developed as we talked with her and as she became involved in a church. But the starting point for her was through encountering God, not through understanding him. And that encounter came through our relationship with her and through her learning to pray – it did not come through our preaching to her. I am not saying that preaching is wrong or that it isn't important. Neither am I saying that people can grow in their faith without being taught the truths of Scripture. What I am saying is that, for the poor, the starting point of faith is often an encounter with God rather than an intellectual grasp of truth.

I recall Jackie Pullinger, for whom I have the highest respect, speaking about her early years in the Walled City in Hong Kong.[7] She shared how, for several years, she focused her efforts on telling people 'the gospel' but saw no fruit whatsoever. Then one day God spoke to her about her approach, challenging her not to preach to people but to love them, and that is what she began to do. Through the love she showed people met with Jesus, and out of that has emerged one of the most amazing ongoing stories of addicts set free, of broken lives restored to wholeness, of people reconnected with the compassionate, living God.[8]

Because all people are made in the image of God, all people need to be reconnected with him if they are truly going to experience transformation in their lives. Transformation cannot come simply through helping people with employment, health, or any other area of physical or emotional wellbeing. Although transformation certainly includes these areas, it only truly comes when people grasp that their identity is in being God's children and that their vocation is to respond to his love for them. Our love for God is not the starting point; it is the response to his love for us. As the writer of 1 John records, 'This is love: not that we loved God, but that he loved us and sent his Son as an atoning sacrifice for our sins.'[9] People therefore need to grasp this wonderful truth. They are made in God's image and, because of this, God loves them and places a value on them that means they are priceless. People grasp this not as an intellectual concept but deep within themselves, when others demonstrate that love to them. Telling people about God's love for them is not nearly as powerful as demonstrating that love.

I came to realize that God is eagerly waiting for the poor to turn to him for help. When they pray God is not dispassionate and distant. Rather, he is like a parent who looks out of the bedroom window eagerly awaiting the return of his son or daughter from a night out. God leans over the world in anticipation that the poor, oppressed and ostracized will simply call on him – and, when they do, he will come. He does not come to force his way, to go against the will of individuals, but he comes to share their pain and to intervene on their behalf. One of my favourite stories from the Gospels, partly because of its simplicity, is the story of one leper who fell at Jesus' feet and pleaded to be healed, 'Lord, if you are willing, you can make me clean.' And Jesus' response is, 'I am willing. Be clean!'[10] Ivan Raskino, who shared at a staff meeting early on during our time in Mumbai, brought this simple story alive for me as he invited us to understand the willingness of God to come to the aid of those who suffer. Therefore, he reminded us, we should always persevere when we pray and never give up.

Praying Is the Place of Weakness

When we choose to humbly pray with people rather than preach at them we choose the place of weakness rather than strength. When people preach they are in a position of strength because they are telling people what the answer is to their situation or predicament. When people pray with another they put themselves in a position of weakness because they are relying on God to do something – to answer that prayer. When we pray with another person we are, in many ways, saying that the difficulty is beyond our capacity to meet and that relief will only come if God intervenes.

There are many mysteries surrounding prayer – why God answers some prayers, for instance, and appears not to answer others,[11] but I have found that there is a dynamic to prayer when we pray among, or on behalf of, those who are oppressed that is often lacking in other more sanitized situations. When we have sought God for the release of a woman who has been trapped in prostitution or for a child who has grown up on the streets and has suffered abuse or when we have prayed for someone who is dying from HIV, we have experienced the closeness of God in a way that I have not known when praying for my own rather petty needs. My most extraordinary experiences of God's presence have occurred when I have been gathered amongst the poor and oppressed to pray. It is incredibly humbling when someone who has faced injustice, who has been let down on numerous occasions, and whose life has been traumatized, raises his or her voice in prayer. Often the measure of faith and hope these people possess is palpable. It is a blessing and an encouragement.

Authenticity in Prayer

Part of the power of these experiences must stem from the authenticity in the prayers of those whose lives are characterized by a hand-to-mouth existence, who need to pray 'Give us today our daily bread.'[12] They do not have that materialistic façade that creates distance between people and that thrives on our personality and image culture in the West. Because there is authenticity in their relationships with others, it carries over into how they relate to God. I sometimes wonder whether the lack of depth in my own praying reflects, to some degree, the shallowness of the culture of which I am a part.

Jesus once told a parable about authenticity in prayer.[13] It was also about humility and self-righteousness. In it Jesus contrasted the prayer of a Pharisee with that of a tax collector, and he told the parable because there were some present who actually believed they didn't need God's help. That is truly incredible. I have never come across a marginalized person who thinks he or she is righteous – all without exception know that they need God. It is those who have power and resources and knowledge who more easily slip into thinking that they can do it on their own. This is certainly true in my own life. As we have seen, in general the poor don't find it difficult to acknowledge their sin. What they do sometimes find difficult to acknowledge, however, is their value as human beings. In this parable the tax collector just asks for God's mercy, and that is all – simple, straightforward, authentic.

In his commentary on this parable, Kenneth Bailey[14] makes the point that the context in which the parable is set and which would have been understood by Jesus' hearers is not private prayer but public worship – a morning or evening atonement sacrifice at the temple. This is the gathered community where the playing field is level, as it were, and all come because all know their personal and collective need for atonement. It is so much more striking, then, that the Pharisee should pray in the manner in which he did. Bailey also makes the point that, while folding one's arms across one's chest was a normal stance in prayer, beating one's chest was highly unusual – especially among men. Because of this, in addition to his bowed head and distance from the others, the sense Jesus conveys is that the tax collector truly knows how much he needs God.

I am not into legalism (in fact quite the opposite), and I know that when we create structures and systems there is always a temptation to become legalistic. One thing we insisted on when we began working in Mumbai, though, was that once a week everyone would meet together early in the morning to pray for a couple of hours. This could have easily become a legalistic require-ment and, had that happened, it would have lost its power. Somehow, however, we managed to avoid that. Each week we all joined together to share our joys, to give thanks for our successes and to lift our needs to God. It was the backbone of all we did. If we think we can make a difference without prayer, then we do not understand the nature of the battle we face. On countless occasions we interceded on behalf of those we served, and on countless occasions we then witnessed God working in their lives. Without those two hours – which for some were quite costly as it meant getting up at five o'clock in the morning – I do not believe we would have witnessed the transformation we were privileged to see.

> Because all people are made in the image of God, his ears are atten-tive to the cries of all people. When those who are poor cry out to him, he hears. When others cry out to him on their behalf, he hears.

10

Receiving

> Perhaps it was more important for me to receive from the
> poor the many gifts born of their love than to try to make
> myself valuable in their eyes.
>
> – *Henri Nouwen*[1]

As I sat on the edge of the only *charpoi* (string bed) in that
slum hutment in Chembur, Mumbai holding John – who
a couple of years previously had come to work on a new
project we were setting up – I realized I would never
fully understand or appreciate his pain or predicament.
I had wanted to do more for him, but because of the
busyness of my own life I had seen him less than I had
intended. At least I had this one last opportunity before

he died to let him know
again that God was with
him in this final challenge.
Over the previous six
months I had witnessed
the quiet and unseen work
of the HIV virus as it left
him defenceless against
even a common cold and
brought him to death's

Because all people are made in the
image of God, all people possess
the capacity to be givers as well as
receivers, to be teachers as well as
learners. We learn much from the
poor – even from those who are
broken and scarred beyond recognition.

door time and again, only to then give yet another brief respite. This time, however, was different. John had turned the final page and, as life ebbed from his frail body, it was time to remember so much that was good in his life and all that I had learnt from our friendship.

John had had a reasonable upbringing in a large family and was given the opportunity of schooling that was denied to so many others in his country. When he was a teenager, circumstances led him into the dark paths of the underworld. John had been picked up by the police, beaten for nothing and then kept in a cell with real criminals. These criminals had held up a vision of easy money that seemed so attractive to a young man who had experienced the corruption of the police first-hand and who desired to make something of his life. And so he got sucked into a world that promised so much but delivered very little.

After being involved in crime and violence for several years that, of course, left their scars, he made a break and came to personal faith in Jesus. He then began to fight a new set of battles, including alcoholism and other enemies within that kept him from a place of stability he so desperately desired. We employed him to help set up a new project to provide training for boys from the slums. He soon became an expert in screen printing.

He then became ill and needed to get his TB (a constantly recurring problem) checked out. It was just before Christmas, and he was due to stay with us over those few days of celebration. On Christmas Eve he brought the medical test results to me as he didn't understand what they meant. I was surprised to see that they had done an HIV test – not because it was not required, but because John was unaware that they'd tested him for HIV. I felt myself go numb when I saw it was positive. I couldn't speak. The next day, Christmas Day 1998, I shared the result with John and talked about the inevitable consequences – unless, of course, God healed him. We hoped and prayed for this kind of healing with all those among whom we worked. His reaction was calm and full of faith. It wasn't that he was expecting a miracle, but he knew that Jesus would be with him regardless of what the HIV infection did to his body.

Over the next year John was up and down. He was admitted to several places for his alcohol addiction but never lasted any course. About a year after this he was out on the streets, living in the entrance way to one of the large city church buildings. Every Sunday he went to church and raised his arms in praise of God. I met with him occasionally, until those final few months when he needed to be hospitalized. He knew what was happening; he knew that his days on earth were numbered; he knew that his dreams of a settled life and marriage were not going to materialize. Yet he remained full of hope, full of faith, full of loving concern for those who had become his friends. He was the teacher, and I was the student. He taught me about faith and perseverance in unbelievable circumstances. He taught me about love and forgiveness. He taught me about thankfulness.

John was just one of the many people whom I count as friends and who, though poor in the eyes of the world, are rich in faith, love and hope. Before entering into the lives of the poor I never appreciated that I was the one who would be blessed. I never could have imagined how much poverty I had to discover in my own life, even in my soul. Unfortunately for many people who view those in need from afar this just doesn't seem plausible. The concept is so upside down that they can't get their heads around it. As Mark Labberton so rightly says, you won't find out unless you take the risk to do so.

Giving love away can seem scary to us. If we love, our world of scarcity says we may lose. No imagination there. So we better love those who will love us back, who show the means to do that. This often leads to the false and distorted conclusion that loving those who suffer, who face injustice, who are in pain or some kind of need means we will be the losers, and we simply can't run that risk. In the vulnerable place many of us live, this cultural pattern seems plainly evident.[2]

Taking that risk, though, is worth more than you could ever imagine. I have never been more deeply fulfilled or known the presence of God with more amazing intensity than when among the ostracized and marginalized.

Meeting God Among the Poor

Many of us have gathered with large crowds in grand auditoriums and sung the latest worship songs with thousands, but this cannot compare with the deep sense of God's awesome presence when sharing tea with a family who doesn't know where their next meal is coming from or holding a child who is dying of HIV. I suppose this shouldn't surprise me, because so many have discovered how God often uses those who are broken and marred and scarred and poor to teach those who think they are whole about some deeper issues. A few people who have discovered this truth have expressed their thoughts as follows:

I found that I was just as likely to meet God in the sewers of the ghetto as in the halls of academia. I learnt more about God from the tears of the homeless mothers than any systematic theology ever taught me.[3]

I discover that I am learning many new things, not just about the pains and struggles of wounded people, but also about their unique gifts and graces. They teach me about joy and peace, love and care and prayer – what I could never have learned in any academy. They also teach me what nobody else could have taught me, about grief and violence, fear and indifference. Most of all, they give me a glimpse of God's first love, often at moments when I start feeling depressed and discouraged.[4]

This is the experience of many who discover that, among the poor, the image of God is never hidden completely. If we keep an open heart and mind we might discover God's image reflected among the poor in ways that we would not expect. The pages of the New Testament seem to reflect this, too. A poor widow teaches us about generosity, a prostitute about love, a sick woman about faith. All were from the margins of society, rejected without cause, yet Jesus holds them up as examples of true spirituality.

The Poor Teach Us About Faith

Where would you turn today to learn about faith? To a well-known preacher or healer? Many do, thinking that faith is exercised on the stages of big arenas. The majority of us in the Western church understand faith within a specific framework that says we have rights and that security and comfort are the norm. For the poor, faith is often a hand-to-mouth affair, an all-encompassing focus on survival, not comfort. These are the people who can and do teach us about faith's true meaning. If we want to know about faith, we have to turn to the poor. The writer of James was greatly concerned that faith should not just be about what we believe, but that it should involve what we do and say as well. He says, 'Has not God chosen those who are poor in the eyes of the world to be rich in faith and to inherit the kingdom he promised those who love him?'[5] This verse is found in the middle of a passage in which James is obviously seeking to overcome the bias and favouritism of those in the church who would treat the poor with discrimination and only give the good seats to the rich. His point is that those who seem to be of little value in the eyes of the world are actually those who have a special place in God's heart. They possess within themselves the capacity for tremendous levels of faith and will find a place in his eternal kingdom.

I used to think that this passage in Scripture merely meant that it was easier for the poor, without the distractions of material possessions, to commit themselves to follow Jesus. Experience in India taught me that there is truth in this but, beyond that, it is also true that those who are poor demonstrate faith more openly and truly in their everyday lives. When I pray for someone who is not well, I always know that, if God does not heal this person, I have the financial resources to take him or her to the hospital. When a poor person prays for someone, they put their total trust in God. Without any financial resources, they can only trust in God. When options apart from God are taken away from people, greater faith is often the result.

One time some of the street children at the side of Kandivili station in Mumbai were talking about how God had been with them that past week. One boy shared how he and his friend had been on a train and, because of the sheer numbers of people, they had become separated from one another (which is not hard to do in a train during Mumbai's rush hour). He had prayed that Jesus would somehow reunite them. At the next station he got off and was immediately arrested for not having a ticket. (Street children would usually travel on the trains without tickets, so this was not unusual.) When he was taken to the railway police office, he was amazed to see his friend there. He had also been arrested for not having a ticket. His prayer, he said, had been answered.

Generosity

In 2 Corinthians 8 the lesson is different, but the principle is the same. Here Paul is urging the church in Corinth to be generous as he says, 'see that you also excel in this grace of giving' (v. 7). He points out the incredible generosity of the Macedonian churches, who gave towards the needs of the brothers in the Jerusalem church. Paul makes a point of telling the Corinthian church that the generosity of those in the Macedonian churches came not out of their wealth but out of their poverty. In addition to that, he mentions the joy they had experienced in the midst of a very severe trial.

> And now, brothers and sisters, we want you to know about the grace that God has given the Macedonian churches. Out of the most severe trial, their overflowing joy and their extreme poverty welled up in rich generosity. For I testify that they gave as much as they were able, and even beyond their ability. Entirely on their own, they urgently pleaded with us for the privilege of sharing in this service to the saints.[6]

Caroline lived near the church we ran in Waterloo, and her daughter Leanne attended the kids' programme there. She was an alcoholic and had become a single parent when her husband took his own life. Since then she had tried desperately hard and fought bravely to bring up her daughter on her own. Things had not gone well, and she ended up losing her house and living in a friend's flea-infested apartment.

It was while things were at their worst for her that she phoned Pete, who oversaw the youth programme at the church. She told him she had a gift for him. Pete had only known her for a few months, but she had often called in to see him and his wife and share something of her pain and struggle. Caroline had once brought Pete a couple of old books as gifts, so Pete knew she had a generous heart and he encouraged her to drop in that day. He was touched that she was thinking of him. When she arrived she said, 'I love what you are doing with the children and young people in this community and I want to give you some money to say thank you and to help those that need it.' She handed him an envelope, which she said he couldn't open until she was gone. Then she said, 'You look tired, you and your wife deserve a holiday. I want you to have this and use it to go some place nice.' And she handed him a second envelope. Pete told me that, if anyone deserved a holiday, it was Caroline, but out of respect and because she was painfully adamant, he accepted the two envelopes. When she left he opened the second envelope that she had said was for a holiday, expecting to find a couple of £10 notes inside. It contained £500. The envelope for the youth work contained £1000. Pete was speechless. He had never received such a generous, sacrificial gift.

I do not think it is going too far to say that the most amazing generosity happens not in circumstances where people live in plenty, but rather in circumstances of poverty. When Jesus pointed to an example of generosity, he talked about a woman who gave two small coins.[7] The point was not only that she gave all she had, but also that she gave out of her poverty. She was a widow and would probably not have had a source of regular income but would have been dependent on the generosity of others. The wealthy might give larger gifts, but they have much more left over. I have received gifts from those who live in plenty and I appreciate their generosity very much. I have also sought to be generous with my own wealth. Yet I know that even the most sacrificial gift I have ever given does not come within a mile of the generosity of the poor, of which I have so often been the recipient. I have been with people in a slum community who struggle to find enough resources to send one of their four children to school, and yet they have gone out to buy a chicken for dinner simply because I came to visit. One time as I approached a tiny hutment that would probably not survive the monsoon rains and would have greatly benefited from the purchase of some plastic sheeting, one of the children was sent off to buy cold drinks and snacks for us, their guests. What generosity we witness at the feet of those who have so little. Indeed, it is we who are 'rich' who learn about generosity through the lives of the poor.

In 2 Corinthians 8 Paul also says that the people in the Macedonian churches experienced 'overflowing joy' in the midst of their poverty and trial (v. 2). Would you expect to find joy in situations of suffering and trial? If you want an answer to that, you only need to compare the majority of congregations in the wealthy West with congregations in the slums and favelas and barrios of the global South. I have witnessed the greatest demonstrations of praise and thankfulness among the poor – with no inhibitions, no correct ways of expression, no formality coming into God's presence. Pure, raw thankfulness comes from the hearts of people who are conscious of their utter dependence on God in the midst of the daily toil and despair of circumstances they did not create, situations they did not choose. The poor know the meaning of joy. The person who wins a million dollars from the lottery really hasn't begun to understand the depth of true joy. Any celebration that occurs at the unexpected luck of a jackpot set of numbers is at best temporal and at worst divisive. The joy of the poor as they experience the presence of the eternal God in the midst of their poverty is overwhelming. There are no words that can describe it. Those who are lucky enough to witness such joy never forget the experience. Sushila taught us about this on more than one occasion.

Learning About Joy

One day Sushila was telling us about the difficulties she faced owing to the lack of water in the slum where she lived. It had been two weeks since any water had come other than such a tiny trickle that nobody could fill even the smallest water jug. We prayed, and she did too. The next day she came back to tell us what had happened. She was there in the slum when the water started to come. It began ever so slowly but was soon like a rushing river, gushing out of the narrow pipe with such force that the women all stood back in disbelief. 'It's come, it's come!' Sushila exclaimed. No one had an explanation as to what had happened. The community just could not understand how water could come in such abundance. Sushila knew, though, and she told everyone else why. 'It's because Auntie prayed!' she shouted. (Sushila referred to my wife Joan as 'Auntie'.) 'Auntie's God has given us this water!' She danced and laughed and enjoyed a wonderful party with everyone there – simply because there was water gushing out of a small pipe in the middle of a slum. Now that is joy.

Scripture points us to the poor as a source of faith, generosity and joy. It is in their midst that we who are surrounded with so much learn the true value of the things that we take for granted. How can the Western church fall for a gospel of prosperity when so many of our brothers and sisters throughout the world, while faithfully following Jesus, find that they need to exercise faith on a daily basis just concerning their next meal? The prosperity gospel makes a mockery of their experience. Yet, at the same time, their joy makes a mockery of our prosperity. Did not Jesus tell his disciples to pray for their daily bread? When we recite that prayer we forget that Jesus taught it because the majority of those who followed him around Palestine faced that issue each day. We might think the Lord's Prayer somewhat antiquated (at least the bit about 'daily bread'), forgetting that the vast majority of those who pray the prayer today do so needing exactly that provision from God as they pray. The prayer reminds many of us that everything we have comes from God; for the poor the prayer expresses the need of the moment.

Those who work among the poor need to be ready to learn from them – to see God imaged in a way that we may not have seen before. Those who do not have the material possessions that we have may well have hidden resources of love or faith or joy that flow from their innermost being. Not only have those who are poor been made in the image of God in equal measure with those who are rich but, somehow, as the poor become reconnected with their Creator they possess the potential to reflect God's image to the world in a way that we who are comparatively rich, educated and powerful find harder. I do not fully understand this, but there is truth in the fact that education, possessions, and power can actually be a hindrance to our being able to reflect God in our world. Perhaps it has something to do with the simplicity of what faith and love really are in their very essence. Possessions, education and power can somehow make faith and love more complex than they should be and so hide, more than reveal, the God who is love. I suppose this makes sense when we ponder the way that God has chosen to reveal himself and his love to us. As Henri Nouwen says,

> Sitting there among all those handicapped and non-handicapped 'nuts', jumping up and down, singing, laughing, clapping hands, and praying, it suddenly struck me that the poor had gathered the rich around them from all over the world and revealed to them the true love of God. Thus the distinction between handicapped and normal, poor and rich, inefficient and efficient were dissolved, and the basic unity of all who live in the house of God was made visible. 'Irrelevant' lives had acquired a divine relevance, the relevance of a God who is revealed to us in the weakness of a small child, an itinerant preacher, and a crucified outcast.[8]

Being a Servant

Those of us who seek to serve and also to learn from the disenfranchised as we work among them face something of a dichotomy. A servant usually gives and gives and continues to give, because that is required of him. If we serve with an expectation that we are going to receive, then we might end up with a fairly twisted motivation. If we go as servants and never realize that it is the poor who have so much to teach us, then we miss part of God's learning path. Somehow we must remain servants who possess a learning posture; we must seek to give and yet understand that we will receive in abundance. Maybe it is here that Jesus' words 'It is more blessed to give than to receive'[9] truly make sense. Those who serve will find their cup filling up and overflowing. These words don't simply mean that you'll enjoy giving gifts to others more than receiving them. Rather, this truth reflects the way that God has made us as human beings. The greatest blessing in life is to contribute, to use our gifts, and to make a difference in the lives of others.

Because all people are made in the image of God, all people possess the capacity to be givers as well as receivers, to be teachers as well as learners. We learn much from the poor – even from those who are broken and scarred beyond recognition.

Fulfilment comes not from consumption but from service. And that is why, if you choose to enter the lives of the poor, you will never lose out. It is also why those who are poor are often so joyful, because joy comes not from possessing but from giving.

11

Celebration

Earn much, consume little, hoard nothing, give generously,
celebrate life.

– Viv Grigg[1]

God is the God of joy, laughter and fun. Even amidst some
situations of degradation and oppression where pain and
suffering are very real, we have an inbuilt need to create
something of beauty, to celebrate the little joys of life in
some small way. Rich or poor, we all need to celebrate – it
is a part of what it means to be made in God's image. It's
interesting that at times of celebration there is almost
always a level playing field
– even in societies that are
built on inherent inequality,
where the family you were
born into determines how
others perceive you as well
as how you perceive your-
self. There is something
about a festival that creates
a brotherhood in people
that can transcend even
caste and culture.

When God made all people in his
image he celebrated, saying, 'It is
good – very good!' Inherent in our
very nature as those made in God's
image is a yearning for joy, laughter and fun – a longing to celebrate. Among the poor every small
step, every battle won, every
progress made is an opportunity
for a party.

In June, the UK celebrates the Queen's official birthday with the pomp and pageantry of 'Trooping the Colour' at Horse Guards Parade in London. This year the Duke of Edinburgh accompanied the Queen from Buckingham Palace in an ivory-mounted carriage built in 1842. Following an inspection of the troops, she was escorted down the Mall by marching bands and then took the salute from a fly past of Royal Air Force aircraft from the balcony of the palace. There was a royal gun salute at the Tower of London followed by private celebrations with the family. It is always a magnificent occasion costing millions of pounds.

I do not think, however, that the Queen enjoys the day any more than Bablu, Sheelat, Eunice or Uma have enjoyed their own birthday celebrations. All of the women and children living at the AIDS care facility we set up for those who have been ostracized from their communities because of their HIV-positive status have enjoyed their special days as well. The simple celebration of a cake, singing and games can bring unbelievable joy to those who have both suffered and witnessed the suffering of others. To see the eyes of a child light up in amazement at the sight of their birthday cake is a joy to behold. One doesn't need great wealth to celebrate – it can be done with the simplest of resources. In fact, I have come to understand that joy is most evident, most tangible, most meaningful, most joyful (if it can be put like that), in the midst of pain and suffering. When life is tough, when work is monotonous, when drudgery is the order of each and every day, then the occasional respite, the occasional day of celebration, provides a remarkable contrast. Those who are most deprived experience joy most deeply.

In his book *The Irresistible Revolution*, Shane Claiborne documents an unusual celebration that he and others involved in the 'Simple Way' organized on Wall Street in downtown New York. It was to be a 'Jubilee' celebration that was motivated in part by a successful lawsuit that prevented the police from constantly arresting the homeless who lived in that vicinity. The $10,000 that had been received as a payment from the lawsuit was changed into coins and freely distributed to all and sundry. Shane Claiborne describes what he and Sister Margaret stood up to say as the celebration began,

> Some of us have worked on Wall Street, and some of us have slept on Wall Street. We are a community of struggle. Some of us are rich people trying to escape our loneliness. Some of us are poor folks trying to escape the cold. Some of us are addicted to drugs, and others are addicted to money. We are a broken people who need each other and God, for we have come to recognize the mess that we have created of our world and how deeply we suffer from that mess. Now we are working together to give birth to a new society within the shell of the old. Another world is possible. Another world is necessary. Another world is already here.[2]

What a great way to begin a party – and party they certainly did that day. All of us need milestones in our lives that give us opportunities to celebrate – birthdays, graduations, anniversaries. The poor are no different. God created all of us with the capacity for joy and to celebrate the life that God has given each of us.

Everyone Should Have a Birthday

As we've seen, many street children come to the cities of our world either to escape abuse at home or to explore the lure of the bright lights. Often it is a bit of both. Some arrive in the city not knowing or remembering their birthdays and so don't know how old they actually are. Chottu, whom we met in Chapter 4, lived with three others from the streets in a small house in Charkop – the first home for street children that Oasis opened, together with an organization called 'Apna Ghar'. When we realized that none of them knew the days they were born, we decided to give each of them a 'birthday'. No child should go through life without the celebration that a birthday brings! We placed numbers written on small pieces of paper in one bag and the months of the year in another. Each child picked out a piece of paper from each of the two bags – and that became the day their birthday would be celebrated each year. All we had to decide was how old they were going to be the next time that date came around!

A few years later Phil and Rachel, who led an Oasis project for street children on Thane station, arranged an anniversary celebration for the children. Each of the twenty children aged eight to fourteen came to the day centre for a haircut, shower and change of clothes before having a meal in a nice restaurant. For a few hours these children were able to forget the trauma of their daily lives and celebrate with abandon. For those few hours, in their bright new clothes and polished hair, they were unrecognizable to the world – nobody else in the restaurant knew where their home was and where they would return a few hours later.

But among the poor we don't limit ourselves to celebrating only birthdays, anniversaries and festival days. Each day the person who hasn't been employed for years keeps a job, each day without drink for the one who has been addicted, each girl who chooses to leave the brothels, each street child who makes a small decision for their good – these are all cause for praise. There is much to celebrate and to be thankful for on a regular basis.

Celebrating People's Work

The launch of a photo exhibition at the Clocktower Arts Centre in Croydon, South London was a time of celebration, most notably for eight young people connected with the Oasis Foyer in that part of town. The Foyer was set up eight years ago to provide temporary accommodation for young people aged between eighteen and twenty-five who find themselves homeless. The Foyer actually provides much more than just accommodation, as each resident receives assistance to access employment or further education, to move on to independent living, and to rebuild their lives.

The exhibition was organized as the culmination of a short training course in photography run by Hazel Thomson, a professional photojournalist. Kate, the person who organized the whole venture, asked Hazel to be involved. But Hazel was only persuaded to give her time to the project after she met Achol, one of the young people who was interested in doing the course. Through the course the young people learned about the use of colour, light and darkness, as well as how to frame a picture and tell a story through stills. They were then set free to take photos and develop a small portfolio. None of them had ever experienced the joy of seeing others appreciate something that they had created.

At the launch of the exhibition, each of the young artists had a chance to talk about their work and then to see the invited guests appreciate what they had done. Many people from the community and further afield also visited the exhibition in the weeks following. Once the exhibition was over I met with Achol and Shawn, another of the young photographers. Shawn had grown up in Croydon and was living in another hostel at the time. Achol, who was originally from the Sudan, had arrived in Croydon a few years earlier via Saudi Arabia. I watched both their faces light up as they shared not only some of the photos they had taken but also the impact that the whole experience had had on them. Shawn said that, for him, the course had been life changing, while Achol said that she had never felt so important and valued. She shared how she had developed new relationships with local people through the experience. Some of them now recognized her when she walked down the high street and, because of a feature on the exhibition run by the local paper, she'd discovered she could google her name and find several references. I tried it and, sure enough, her name came out top. The experience has motivated and empowered both of these young people as they begin to make choices about their futures.

During our discussion Shawn told me that on one occasion while he was out taking photos he was approached by a couple of policemen who wanted to find out what he was doing. They didn't think his explanation was good enough so they arrested him, took his camera, and handcuffed him. He called Hazel, who was in the vicinity. She explained what it was all about and Shawn was allowed to go free. Though the police were invited to the exhibition launch, sadly they didn't come.

One of the most memorable days for our staff team in India was the fashion show we held in Mumbai.[3] Luke and his team spent several months preparing for the show, and on the night socialites and dignitaries, including the State Minister for Culture, attended. Professional models gave their time free of charge and strode down the catwalk alongside some youngsters who had had only a few weeks of practice. The show highlighted the work of those who made the garments in the manufacturing unit of our Jacobs Well project that served the needs of disadvantaged women in the city. The project, which had been set up by Ruth Cox several years earlier, provided training to a high standard which then enabled women to access the job market. Through the training course women learnt pattern cutting as well as tailoring so some were eventually able to run their own businesses.

The clothes modelled at the show had been specially designed by Amanda King who, together with Ruth (who was back in the UK), was using this as an opportunity to promote the issue of fair trade. If you have ever attended a fashion show you will know that the climax, at the end of the show, is always the appearance of the designer. However at the end of this show, instead of the designer, the five girls who had actually cut the patterns and made the clothes appeared from back stage – to rapturous applause. All of these girls had come from poor backgrounds, and their faces were a picture to behold. Eight hundred people, including politicians, millionaires and some whose autographs were hot property, stood and applauded these five young women who were unknown outside their small communities and who were all seeking to overcome the challenges of poverty. I like to think that Amurtha, who was sixteen and grew up with an alcoholic and abusive father and lived in a very poor community, and Babamma, who had dropped out of school very early and whose marriage had been arranged at sixteen, represented not just all the women at Jacobs Well but all the women of the world who have faced the odds stacked against them. It's hard to imagine a more meaningful celebration than that.

The Bible is full of celebration, too. It's hard to keep track, in fact, of all the festivals celebrated in Leviticus, Numbers and Deuteronomy. Each festival was an important milestone in the life and history of the people of God, and each one provided the people with an opportunity to rest from their work and focus on the bigger picture. Times of celebration help us to do that. And, when the Old Testament mentions festivals and celebrations, there is often a reminder that at those times the people should not forget the alien, the stranger and the widow.

When Jesus arrives on the scene, far from dampening the spirits, he is accused of going over the top with the eating and drinking. Eugene Peterson nicely phrases Jesus' response to this accusation,

> How can I account for the people of this generation? They're like spoiled children complaining to their parents, 'We wanted to skip rope and you were always too tired; we wanted to talk but you were always too busy.' John the Baptizer came fasting and you called him crazy. The Son of Man came feasting and you called him a lush. Opinion polls don't count for much, do they? The proof of the pudding is in the eating.[4]

Prior to these accusations Jesus, as you know, rescued a family from extreme embarrassment when the wine ran out at their wedding. At first Jesus appeared to be a little reticent to get involved, even at his mother's request, but when the servants did what he suggested they discovered a new supply of high quality wine. Jesus' presence certainly livened up the party.

Throwing Parties for the Poor

On another occasion Jesus suggested that the religious
leaders should be throwing parties – not for each other,
but for the poor, blind, crippled and lame. Jesus made
these remarks after he observed guests seating themselves at the places of honour at the table. He then went
on, in response to another remark, to tell a parable in
which those who were invited to a banquet excused
themselves and the poor, crippled, blind and lame took
their places.[5] Those who are poor are often the most
responsive, and they will be found at that great feast in
heaven. Jesus then told three more parables – they are all
about loss and are found in a section of Luke's Gospel
that has sometimes been called the section for the poor.
Each of these parables makes the point that, as people
turn their lives around and begin to follow God's
agenda for their lives on earth, there is rejoicing in the
heavenly realms. While many have seen the recovery of
what was lost as the common thread running through
these parables, another common theme is the ensuing
celebration.

God invented joy, laughter, fun and celebration. He
placed that capacity in us when he made us in his image.
We were not made for monotony, for dreariness or for
boredom – we were made to celebrate as God himself
did when he first created us. And joy is not something to
be kept to oneself – it is a shared experience. When we
receive the good news that we've passed our exams, the
joy comes not from reading the letter but from telling our
family and friends. The God who created laughter and
fun also created community as the context in which these
gifts would be shared.

Those who are poor need to celebrate just as they need
to breathe. As Ray Bakke says,

The urban poor are not well served by bare walls and skimpy decorations. Precisely because their communities may be ugly, their possessions few, and their identities unclear, they need colors, festivals, and celebrations.[6]

> When God made all people in his image he celebrated, saying, 'It is good – very good!' Inherent in our very nature as those made in God's image is a yearning for joy, laughter and fun – a longing to celebrate. Among the poor every small step, every battle won, every progress made is an opportunity for a party.

Celebration is an important part of life for us all. Without it, life is barren. It's easy in the routine of the everyday to forget to stop and celebrate, to thank God for the small mercies of life we often take for granted.

12

Prevention

As God calls us to seek justice, he bids us to equip ourselves with some basic knowledge of what it takes to pursue the call with excellence.

– Gary Haugen[1]

Sona, who is sixteen years old, grew up in a village in the state of Karnataka, South India. With pressure from her family to find work and not many opportunities locally, she took up the offer from a woman who befriended her and offered her a good opportunity in the city of Mumbai, hundreds of miles away. The woman explained that, with the rates of pay much higher in a city than in the rural areas, she would be able to earn enough to live well and send some money back to her family in the village.

The woman brought her to the suburbs of Mumbai where they stayed for a few days. During that time Sona sensed that something was not right and she began to wonder whether the woman was making arrangements to sell her

> All people are made in the image of God. When we prevent that image from being marred through abuse and injustice we are doing God's work.

into prostitution. During those first few days Sona met Raj, who lived with a relative of the woman who was trafficking her. Sona talked with Raj about her unease and her concern as to whether she was to be sold into prostitution. Raj then contacted Oasis, and our investigation team sent a social worker on a surprise visit to the house where Sona was staying. She was rescued before the sale took place and has stayed in Mumbai. She is presently enrolled on a beautician's course.

Sadam and Iqbal, both aged nine, and Mithun, aged thirteen, are all children from different villages in the State of Bihar in North India where poverty is rife and opportunity is scarce. They all met through a 'job agent' who offered to take them to Mumbai where they would be able to work in the hotel industry cleaning tables and washing dishes for Rs1,000 (about $20) a month – enough to live on with some to send home to their families. Their families had all agreed that the boys should go to Mumbai since, in their eyes, there was no other option.

The 'job agent' brought them to Mumbai by train – a journey that takes just over 24 hours. They happened to arrive in Mumbai while our Oasis early encounter team was on the railway station looking out for children who might have been trafficked. The 'job agent', sensing danger on arrival in Mumbai, fled the scene and the three boys were taken to a government safe house where they were followed up by our social workers.

Every day, thousands of people – men, women and children – arrive in Mumbai. They are seeking work, a way to support their families, escape from hardship, a better life. But so many of these people are deceived. They are given a false promise of work and then find themselves enslaved, being forced to work long hours in horrific conditions for little or no pay. Instead of finding a better life, they are trafficked into situations of slavery from which there is little hope of escape.

Sona, Saddam, Iqbal and Mithun were some of the fortunate ones – rescued before any abuse took place. Monisha was less fortunate. Due to a variety of family circumstances, she ended up living with her mother on the streets of the city of Bangalore. Her mother remarried someone who not only failed to care for Monisha but who exploited her in the extreme, making money selling her for sex. He would take her to a building where she would be required to do domestic work and then he'd give her to a man for the remainder of the night. Eventually she found herself in a brothel. She was eleven years old. Her only source of comfort to ease the pain of abuse was to sniff glue. In time that became an addiction.

Not long ago our social workers were talking to a fifteen-year-old girl who, unusually, had recently managed to run away from a brothel and was staying in the Bangalore government home for minors. She had been trafficked four years previously and was able to provide information about her captors. Our staff then undertook some surveillance at several of the locations that she mentioned and organized a raid to be conducted by the police. Two girls were rescued in this raid, Monisha being one of them. She is now in a safe home and is making slow progress, but she has a long journey to full recovery ahead of her.

Of all the evils in our world, human trafficking must rank as one of the most horrendous. Profiting financially from the sale of people into modern slavery is a growing phenomenon around the world. It includes the sexual exploitation of minors as well as the abuse of children in situations of forced labour. And those who work among poor communities quickly discover how vulnerable they are to such exploitation. Trafficking does not affect the middle-class, for it is poverty that drives people to accept the offer of a job miles from home or, in some cases, to sell their children.

If all people are made in the image of God, then our role is not only to care for those who are broken, marred and scarred but also to do what we can to prevent people from experiencing abuse and its resulting brokenness. Sona was fortunate in that she was rescued a few hours or days before being sold into prostitution. She was able to get on with her life without the trauma of being raped and having to serve endless customers night after night. Thousands are less fortunate. Many young girls who are trafficked into prostitution as teenagers are swallowed up into the darkness of nameless identity and often emerge only years later – when the HIV virus has taken its toll or when their bodies are worn out from abuse. And some, of course, die.

For many years we sought to care for girls who had been trafficked into prostitution and to empower them to leave and begin a new life when they decided that they wanted to do so. It was clear, though, that for every girl who chose to leave or was rescued there were many others available to replace them, through the evil of human trafficking. Surely, we decided, it is better to try to prevent the sale of girls in the first place rather than caring only for those who are already victims. So in Oasis we developed a new strategy and are now seeking to intervene and rescue girls prior to their final sale – often a few weeks after they go missing. The strategy involves obtaining information about missing people as quickly as possible, conducting surveillance work along trafficking routes, and intervening with the police when traffickers are being apprehended. In addition to that, our team works with the police and other government authorities to ensure that victims can testify against those involved and that prosecutions are followed through. It is imperative to oppose bail for those who are involved in trafficking so they aren't able to interfere with witnesses. It is only when the law against trafficking is strengthened and increasing numbers of traffickers are prosecuted that we will prevent girls from being caught up in this evil.

The Importance of Early Encounter

One of the key principles on which this anti-trafficking strategy is based is that of early encounter – intercepting situations before they lead to abuse and trauma. In the case of many women who are being trafficked, there is a window of a few weeks between when they are lured or taken and when they are finally sold. Some, of course, are abused immediately after they are taken, but in an Asian context there is often a period of time before that takes place. This principle of early encounter is also applicable to street children. If a street child is encountered on entry into a city, prior to weeks or months of living on the streets, then the chances are far greater of preventing needless suffering. This was true of Shahanaz, whom we met in Chapter 4.

The early encounter strategy is one preventative approach that can be effective in some contexts, but even among street children there are a range of interventions that could be considered even prior to 'early encounter'. Each of these children has come from a home and a community and has left that context for some specific reason. Vishal, for example, comes from a family in a fairly traditional village community some distance away from Mumbai. He was not driven from his home because of abuse – he came to the city because his family wanted him to earn money that they could not earn. He did this by begging on Thane station. He actually earned a considerable amount begging because he had polio in both legs and could not walk. His method of transport was a wooden board on wheels, like a square version of a skateboard. Vishal was twelve years old when I first met him, smart, and a lot of fun. He did not have to beg long each day to earn enough to feed himself, and the rest he kept with a trusted tea-stall owner so that it would not be stolen by the others who lived on the station platform. Every few months he would take his earnings and return home to provide for his family. His income was far in excess of that of our staff members who worked in that project!

For Vishal, a preventative approach would have had to be undertaken back in his village, among his family. If some way could have been found for Vishal's father to earn a decent wage, then maybe Vishal could have stayed with the family and attended his local school. Many others, of course, come to the city because of some measure of family breakdown or abuse. Again, a preventative approach might involve work back in the villages, strengthening the family unit. The challenge, though, is that there are millions of families within a hundred-mile radius of the city – and nobody knows which ones are vulnerable. Early encounter together with family reintegration seems to be the most viable preventative approach when working with limited resources.

One of the boys recently repatriated in India following his rescue from a situation of child labour was asked to idenify the most significant thing that could be done for him in order to ensure that he wouldn't be re-trafficked. His answer? 'A cow!' His view was that, if his family had a cow, it would tremendously aid their sustainability and would go a long way towards him being able to attend school rather than having to work. It's an idea well worth investigating.

We have to think of creative ways to help break the cycles of poverty and injustice in which so many people around the world find themselves trapped. A great example of a small but significant way to bring about change comes from Shakila, a young woman living in Waterloo, on the edge of two notorious boroughs – Southwark and Lambeth. These two boroughs seem to battle each other for the worst statistics. One of these statistics is the frightening number of teenage pregnancies. At one time, in fact, Lambeth had the highest rate of teenage pregnancy in Western Europe. The church there, church.co.uk, wanted the young people to be empowered to do something for themselves. Shakila was seventeen years old when she came up with the idea – and the funding – to run a project for teenage girls in Lambeth who thought they might quite like a baby in the near future. Shakila hired some simulator babies that cry when they need to be fed, when they need to be changed, and just because they want to be held. Five girls were each given a baby to look after for one week and, after a pep talk and explanation from Shakila, they went on their way.

The girls were excited at the beginning of the project. Only two days and two nights later, however, one of the girls was begging Shakila to take the baby off her hands. 'I didn't realize how hard it was,' she complained. 'I thought it would be fun.' One by one the girls all brought the babies back, each with similar stories. Eighteen-year-old Rochelle said, 'I am not gonna have a baby until I'm in a really serious relationship with a man that knows how hard this whole baby thing is. Maybe when I'm thirty I'll be ready.' Shakila also arranged for two girls who worked for Oasis and who had recently given birth to come to answer any questions the girls had. Some of the girls felt that the babies were unrealistic because they kept crying. Suffice it to say, the new mums were able to shed some light on the truth about the difficulty and privilege of raising children.

Raising Awareness

As we seek to address the issue of human trafficking and to help children so that they don't have to live on the streets, one preventative component that is possible and desirable is awareness raising. Communities that are vulnerable to children being lured or forced from home, or where children may choose to leave for the bright lights of the city, can be made aware of the dangers and so guard against them. Raising awareness is a challenge not because of the logistical problems, which can easily be overcome, but because of restrictions placed on funding. Those who fund projects generally want to see the outcomes of their investment and it is just about impossible to demonstrate, in the short-term, the direct impact of awareness raising on either a reduction in children living on the streets or on human trafficking.

Poverty, of course, has many causes, and dealing with issues of poverty is a complex enterprise. The reasons human trafficking occurs or the reasons children end up on the streets are never the same or one-dimensional. In Vishal's situation, for instance, I mentioned that his father needed a job that would provide enough money to support his family. The idea of just providing a job for Vishal's father is somewhat simplistic, as there were many factors that went into the decision that Vishal and his family made for him to live on the streets. These included local community cohesion, cultural views of life and the future, state government and national government policy. It might even have been that international trade agreements played their part. They certainly did in Sonia's case, as we saw in Chapter 7. The demand for cheaply produced clothing and the special status given to Bangladesh in the production of garments have led in the past to exploitation of children in large garment factories. As Bryant Myers reminds us, 'No process of human and social transformation can be entirely defined locally. Every community is part of a family of social systems that are regional, national, and finally global.'[2]

In Christian mission we have traditionally been very good at caring for people – this is a natural outworking of the compassion we believe God has given to us for a world that is suffering and which he loves. We have also been good at dealing with people trapped in poverty at a personal level – working with individuals to escape the web of circumstances in which many people find themselves ensnared. We have become better at understanding how communities operate and how to work with people in their specific community contexts. What we are now beginning to wake up to are the issues at a macro-level that impact the poor – issues like trade policy, unlimited economic growth, ecology, and many others. Each of these is an arena for Christian mission – because how government policies are shaped, how businesses operate, and how we as the public behave will all have an enormous impact on whether future generations around the world are plunged into poverty or not. Raising public awareness with regard to these issues can make a significant difference. The fair trade movement is one example of that. Many people, since they are now more aware of the sources of the coffee, tea, chocolate, and bananas they buy, make choices that assist the poor in other parts of the world. The fair trade movement as a whole has raised awareness, but within it are many organizations that have advocated on behalf of specific producer groups to ensure they receive a fair price for their products. Awareness raising and advocacy go hand-in-hand.

Advocacy Is a Part of Prevention Strategies

Advocacy is about speaking out on behalf of others. It can be carried out at an individual level as one person chooses to represent another person to a third party. This is the legal understanding of the term. On occasions advocacy happens at a local or national level as a person or group of people takes a stand on behalf of another group of people – often when they cannot speak out for themselves.

Jim Wallis, who is based in the United States, has been a powerful voice urging the church to advocate on behalf of the poor. His book *God's Politics* is a call to the church in the USA to put aside old paradigms of engagement and to think differently about how the church can collectively make a difference and build a just and equitable society. It might surprise you to know that, in the USA, one in six children is poor – and that figure rises to one in three among people of colour. Jim has been involved in local community development for many years, but he says that 'Effective local community service and development are not substitutes for advocacy, for supporting good public policy in Washington D.C., and in the States.'[3] As an example of this, he describes how he and many others across the political and religious spectrum jointly sought to advocate on behalf of the poor during the election campaign of 2004. Here is an extract from the 'Unity Statement on Overcoming Poverty' that this group produced.

> In America, people who work should not be poor, but today many are. We must ensure that all people who are able to work have jobs where they do not labor in vain, but have access to quality health care, decent housing, and a living income to support their families. The future of our country depends upon strong and stable families that can success-fully raise their children. We must also ensure that those who are unable to work are cared for by our society. [4]

In Oasis we have joined with many others under the 'Stop the Traffik' banner to speak out on behalf of the victims of human trafficking. Our goal is to bring an end to this evil. One of our very specific targets is to stop the cocoa production companies in the Côte d'Ivoire from harvesting their cocoa through the use of children traf-ficked into the country. The big chocolate companies in the West source 41% of their cocoa from that country, and even today they refuse to ensure that the ingredients they use have not been produced through such abuse. It is estimated that around twelve thousand children have been trafficked into this specific situation.

> Diabate and Traore had left their village in Mali to go to the Ivory Coast looking for enough money to afford a bicycle, but they were sold to a man who had paid 50,000 West African Francs (about $80) for the two boys and wanted the money back – in labour. The boys from Sirkasso met about twenty others in the same predicament and learned that no one was ever paid. They slept in a rectangle-shaped mud hut that initially had windows but when some boys found they could escape during the night, the windows were

sealed shut. Diabate and Traore remember eating mostly bananas, though they would gobble up the cocoa beans, as others did, whenever they got the chance. Many months passed, and the boys forgot what the purpose had once been for this adventure. Life became a struggle to exist, then hardened to despair.[5]

The whole point of this campaign is not simply to help boys like Diabate and Traore be freed from their slavery; it is to prevent another twelve thousand being trafficked in their place – it is to put an end to trafficking. You can imagine how little interest the chocolate industry took when the campaign started. After all, they had managed to get around an agreement they had made with the United States government under the Harkin-Engel protocol to ensure full disclosure from source to sale by 2005. This was then extended to July 2008, but the chocolate industry has again found its way around the implications of this simply by redefining certification. As part of that agreement the chocolate industry was to establish philanthropic activity in communities where the cocoa farms are found. But while there are approximately eighteen thousand such communities, activities have only started in 88 (correct at the time of writing). If the United States government was not going to pursue the enforcement of full disclosure, we wondered, what chance of success did such a little campaign have?

Well, after a couple of years of advocating on behalf of those trafficked onto the cocoa plantations, it is beginning to make a difference. In increasing numbers people are choosing to purchase only fair trade chocolate, and the big players are beginning to see the impact in their sales and profits. Last year Royal Verkade, a Dutch subsidiary of United Biscuits, announced that it would be using 100% fair trade chocolate in its products. This decision, it is estimated, will yield a 20% increase in fair trade chocolate sales in Europe. This year both Cadbury and Mars have announced that they will change a portion of their production to guarantee either fair trade or slave-free chocolate. So, although there is still a long way to go in preventing more children from being trafficked into forced labour on the cocoa farms of the Côte d'Ivoire, progress is being made.

This all happens at a macro-level, but when we approach our work at a grass-roots level we also need to think through how a preventative approach might create more empowerment and greater sustainability. For example, if in a specific community there is an issue with malaria, you might decide to provide coils to keep the mosquitoes away at night. If you do that once, you will have to carry on for years. Alternatively, you might train local community health workers to educate people living in the area about how malaria spreads and what to do to avoid getting it. That would help, but you would still be dealing with the symptoms and not the cause. Another option would be to look at why mosquitoes are drawn to that location in great numbers and work with the community to deal with the pools of stagnant water that attract the mosquitoes in the first place. That approach won't just help those who live there today, it will also help all of those who will live there in the future. It is a preventative approach.

In some measure, every small step towards wholeness for those we work amongst has a preventative outcome because poverty tends to be generational. When a father who didn't have a job becomes employed he has income to send his children to school and, because they have access to education, his children stand a better chance of also accessing jobs that will provide a sustainable livelihood for them and their families. When someone comes to understand that they are created by God, bear his

All people are made in the image of God. When we prevent that image from being marred through abuse and injustice we are doing God's work.

image and have been given a mandate to steward the earth, then it will have an enormous impact not only on them as individuals but also on their children and their children's children.

13

Perspective

> God invites all those who hold such commitments – to
> human dignity, justice, servantheartedness, community,
> inclusion and diversity, holism, participation, hope and his
> presence in the world – to journey together, to work tog-
> ether and to weep together.   – *Malcolm Duncan*[1]

One of the groups of people with whom I became acquainted over our years in Mumbai was the traffic police – an unreached people group if ever there was one. My contact with them was almost exclusively at their instigation, not mine, as they stood near traffic lights and road intersections seeking company. The reasons they stopped me to have a chat were endless. On one occasion I was deemed to have gone

Because all people are made in the image of God, all people are equally precious in his sight. Sin has not simply separated people from him, it has prevented them from being all that God intends. God is at work in the world to see his image fully restored in people. He uses a whole variety of means to achieve this, including among people who do not acknowledge his existence or purposes. As we work to see God's image restored among the poor we do not do so in isolation but as part of the wonderful mosaic of God's work in the world.

the wrong way around a bollard, on another it was due
to the way the number plate was affixed to my scooter.
The most unusual of all was when I was stopped for
pushing my scooter the wrong way down the road, having discovered that a petrol station was closed and that I
needed to go back 50 yards to the previous one!

The traffic police were there, of course, to ensure that
the traffic flowed easily and safely through a very con-
gested city. Because they were underpaid, however, a
large portion of their income came from small donations
from motorists caught breaking traffic rules. These donations ensured that violators wouldn't have their licences
taken away or have to pay the more hefty fines that
would be imposed through official routes. Everyone was
a winner! The motorist got away with paying less and
not having the inconvenience of having to go and collect
his licence from the police station; the traffic policeman
made some extra income, which he badly needed to support his family.

The main problem, though, was that the traffic police
forgot why they were really there and focused almost
entirely on making the extra money they needed. They
became blind to the bigger picture of ensuring a safe and
smooth flow of traffic and focused instead on the smaller issue of making money. In fact, on one occasion I was
travelling along one of the major roads on my scooter
when a vehicle came from the left-hand side and almost
knocked me down. (Since people drive on the left in
India, overtaking is supposed to happen on the right
side of vehicles.) When that happened, I thought to
myself, 'Now where are the police?' Then I realized that
it was a police jeep that had nearly knocked me down.
When people lose sight of the big picture they can so easily miss the real reason for their existence. The Mumbai
traffic police are just an example, but this is a challenge

for all churches and Christian organizations – we can so easily live within our own little world, forgetting that there is a bigger picture. We all need perspective.

Gaining a Wider Perspective

When we began our work in Mumbai, some questioned whether or not there was room for another organization. The underlying view was that there was already so much division of effort, it would be much better if there were fewer but larger entities. There is some merit in this view but, for me, what is more important than the number of organizations in a given location is their approach to working with others. And that approach often stems from people's perspective on their context, on the work they do and on what God is doing in that context. One day, for example, we had a visitor from Canada. We met on a Sunday morning and, after we attended our church service, we took him out for lunch. We then went for a short walk and continued to talk about the work we were doing. This visitor then turned to me and asked a question that I heard frequently. 'Andy,' he said, 'seeing all the need and the fact that you are only helping such a few people, don't you get discouraged?' I had been talking with him about our work among street children and in the slums and brothels that, at the time, was reaching barely a few hundred people – and he had understood a dilemma that many face. When you work in a mega-city with so much that could be done and you are involved with a handful of people, it's tempting to compare the magnitude of the need with the inadequacy of your response. 'Sometimes I do get discouraged,' I told him, 'but that's only when I get caught up in my own world and forget to look at the bigger picture.' I went on to explain. I told him of about ten other organizations and churches that were involved in similar work. I explained a little about the great things that others were doing and concluded by saying that, all together, we were having a significant impact in the city. While Oasis might have been impacting five hundred people, when we multiplied that out by what ACT and Teen Challenge, Intermission, Valley of Praise Church, New Life Fellowship, Bombay Baptist Church and so many others were doing, then the numbers were quite significant. Alone we were helping a few, together we were helping thousands. And it was that perspective, I explained to this visitor, that we sought to carry around in our hearts. When we celebrate the joys and successes of others and let them celebrate ours, we can all celebrate what God is doing.

It is sad yet true that, in many situations, those ministering in the city do not even know what else is happening. They go about their work in isolation and never bother to research what else is happening, let alone connect with it. Many people simply assume that nothing else is happening and stand back in amazement when they discover that God has given similar vision to others. Patrick McDonald, who set up Viva Network, recounts an experience he had when they held a meeting for interested organizations working among children at risk in Argentina. During the course of the introductions, one person stood up and introduced himself as the representative of 'the only prison children's ministry in Cordoba and probably all of Argentina'. The person sitting next to him then stood up and described himself as the representative of the 'second prison children's ministry in Cordoba'.[2] Neither had known before that the other existed. For two people the world became a slightly smaller place that day.

Discouragement

It's easy to lose perspective when we only see what we do and not what others are doing as well. When we lose our perspective we end up thinking that everything depends on us. When we think that it all depends on us and things don't go well (as they won't at times) we become discouraged. When we become discouraged we become less effective. Perspective is an antidote to discouragement and a stimulus to effectiveness.

Although Elijah might have become discouraged more than once, Scripture tells us about one particular occasion in 1 Kings 18–19. Elijah had just seen an incredible manifestation of God's presence and power on Mount Carmel that, one would think, would have stimulated faith to last him a lifetime. The setting was a confrontation between Elijah and the prophets of Baal, and the challenge was whether Baal's or Israel's God could, when called upon, bring fire on the offering of a bull. It was all or nothing for Elijah, and God did not disappoint him as the flames, which had been noticeably absent when the prophets of Baal called on their god, completely consumed the sacrifice that Elijah had prepared. Had God not appeared in such a powerful way, not only would Elijah's ministry have come to an end, but most likely his life as well. It was the ultimate test, and through these events the people began to see for themselves that YHWH was God and God alone. The people of Israel were convinced, and they demonstrated that immediately by obeying Elijah's command to finish off the prophets of Baal. Elijah waited on the top of Mount Carmel, the rains finally came, and God's power then enabled Elijah to run faster than a chariot, in the rain, all the way back to Jezreel.

What happened next was unexpected. Ahab, the king of Israel, reported all of these events to his wife Jezebel,

who vowed to kill Elijah and sent a message to let him
know. (Remember that all of Israel had just gathered on
Mount Carmel and seen the power of God.) The people
were now on Elijah's side, yet for some unknown reason
Elijah became afraid and ran to the desert near Beersheba
and asked God to take his life. God's answer was food
and drink that gave Elijah enough strength to travel
another 40 days and enabled him to arrive at Horeb.
There God asked him what on earth he was doing and
Elijah verbalized his discouragement for a second time.
He had first mentioned it on Mount Carmel, saying to the
people, 'I am the only one of the LORD's prophets left.'
And at Horeb he said the same thing directly to God.
God's answer was a further revelation of his presence
through a still small voice. Immediately following that,
God again asked him what he was doing there and Elijah
repeated what he had said before – that he was the only
one left and that Jezebel had vowed to kill him. At this,
God issued Elijah some instructions that clearly showed
that he is God, sovereignly working at the macro-level in
the lives of kings and rulers. He also provided Elijah with
some much-needed perspective. There were at least
seven thousand others who, like Elijah, were still firm in
their desire to follow God. That was news to him.

What had happened to Elijah? He had witnessed some
wonderful things, but somehow he had lost his perspective. Far from being the only one left, there were seven
thousand others who had not succumbed to the draw of
Baal worship either and who remained, as Elijah did,
faithful to the Lord. Elijah needed to see his own situation and work in a broader light, in the totality of what
God was doing. He needed to know that he wasn't
alone, that there were others who were equally faithful
and seeking to do God's will. He needed to see his part
within the context of the bigger picture.

Collaboration and Partnership

If we view our context in the broader perspective of what God is doing rather than through a narrow lens focused only on what we are doing, we open up a whole range of opportunities. Our 'competitors' become our friends and allies; their resources become ours; we can move from friendship to joint planning and joint action, to collaboration and partnership. Collaboration is a first step. Collaboration is about thinking through how our work can integrate with others and vice versa. Without collaboration, everyone has to think of doing everything. In work with street children, for example, everyone would have to think about detached work, education, rehabilitation, health care, reintegration and a whole range of other things as well. Collaboration, first of all, avoids the nemesis of duplication – the scenario in which there are ten safe houses but nobody engaged in reintegration, or ten programmes for reintegration but no safe houses. Sadly, this sort of thing happens far more often than you might expect, and it happens because people do not think about their context from God's perspective. It always starts with this lack of perspective.

People who work among the poor face temptations on two extremes. Discouragement, as we have noted, is one of them. When our ministry affects only a tiny percentage of those in urgent need, we will be tempted to question the value of what we are doing. The other temptation, though, is to believe that God has revealed his strategy for effectiveness to you, and to you alone. The danger of having some measure of success is that it can lead people to the false belief that they alone are right. This can be very subtle and deceptive. Very often, for obvious reasons, people do not voice this sort of belief – yet they live out their lives on this basis. How we react when we

succeed probably reveals more of what is in our hearts
than how we respond to times of testing. Increasing insu-
larity and self-dependence are two tell-tale signs that
people think they are right and others are wrong. This
can happen to congregations or organizations, and it can
be so subtle that often people don't even realize it's happening. We can become blind to our own pride. Every
time God blesses the work of our hands, we are tempted
to believe that we have got it right and to compare ourselves with the other church or organization that is struggling.

We must stay connected to the whole big picture of
God's work in the context where we live. We must see
what we do in the context of what God is doing. We must
understand that God does not have only one way of
doing things. God has lots of methodologies, lots of
strategies, lots of ways of going about things. This variety
is part of God's overall strategy in building his kingdom.
Just as we understand that each one of the ostracized and
marginalized people that we work amongst are made in
God's image, so we must remember that each person
who works among the poor is likewise made in God's
image. We exhibit true compassion for the poor when we
rejoice as someone is brought to wholeness through the
work of another organization or church. In our line of
work we have no competitors. It is God's work, not ours.

It is not only when we are discouraged that we need
to see the part that God has called us to play in the context of the broader picture of God's kingdom. We also
need to see this when things are going well. When the 72[3]
returned from their short-term outreach in Luke 10, they
were elated to report what they had seen and done. The
highlight for them was the fact that even the demons had
submitted to them when they ministered in the name of
Jesus. Jesus endorsed what had happened, saying that he

himself had witnessed that in the spiritual realm. But then Jesus refocused their attention. This, he reminded them, was not to be the substance of their joy. Rather, they were to rejoice in the fact that they were a part of a wider community of believers who were connected to God, the source of love and power. The source of their joy, Jesus told them, should be that one day they will gather together for eternity to be with the Father. It is easy to get carried away with the successes of our work and lose our focus on the wider kingdom picture. Here Jesus gives that wider picture.

On another occasion the disciples came across someone who was casting out demons in Jesus' name.[4] They reported back to Jesus that they had told this person to stop because he wasn't one of them. Jesus' response was quite incredible. 'Do not stop him,' Jesus said, 'for whoever is not against you is for you.'[5] It is so easy for us to perceive reality the other way round. If people are not with us we tend to assume they are against us. This incident occurred early on in Jesus' ministry. In fact, Luke records it prior to the 72 being sent out on their first outreach experience. Jesus wanted the disciples to learn this lesson sooner rather than later. In essence, Jesus tells them, 'Don't worry so much about the background or foundation of others doing similar work – if they are working in my name, welcome them as fellow ministers.'

What Being 'One' Means in Practice

Jesus placed a high priority on unity. His prayer in John 17 is filled with references to his followers being 'one'. He is referring not just to the 12 or the 72 but to all of those who will believe and follow him in the future.[6] We cannot be one with others unless we see that their work is God-given and significant in its impact in the same context in which we work and minister. We are not talking here about networking, which is an important aspect of methodology. We are talking about being of one spirit with others called to minister in the midst of the same difficulties, joys and challenges. We are talking not just about appreciating what others are doing, but about seeing their church and ministry as spiritually joined to ours. Or maybe we even need to see it the other way round – our ministry being joined to theirs. It is not that we do joint programmes as a superficial demonstration of being Christians together. Rather, it is a mindset that sees all Christians in a town or city, though they are all part of different congregations, as one church. We are all working in the same kingdom for the same Lord and with the same destiny.

When Paul writes to believers in Corinth, he writes to the 'church of God in Corinth'.[7] There might have been many congregations meeting in different homes in the city, but there was one church. When Paul writes to believers in Rome he writes 'To all in Rome who are loved by God and called to be saints.'[8] These believers, too, were scattered throughout the city and came together to worship in different homes, yet they were all part of the one church in that city.

If all people engaged in work among the poor saw themselves as spiritually joined to all of the others ministering in Christ's name, what a difference it would make both in understanding their task and their effectiveness. Everyone could play a part, small as it might seem, while encouraging others to play their small part, knowing that together we are building something significant in kingdom terms. How ridiculous it must seem from a heavenly perspective that we are even tempted to perceive others as competitors – competing for the same funding and resources and even geographical locations. Imagine platoons in an army fighting over where on the front line they will position themselves for the battle.

I recently heard about someone who had done extensive research on the issues of partnership, and one of his conclusions was that partnerships generally work well until they are successful. Often it is when credit is apportioned that disagreements begin to divide. That, unfortunately, was our experience early on when we worked together with another organization among street children in a particular location in Mumbai. We made the mistake of not defining, in sufficient detail, both the boundaries of responsibility and ownership. So when the leader of the other organization suggested that we part company, it was really a request to allow them to carry on the work without us. At that point we had a choice to make. Would we argue and fight or move on and release? We chose the latter, and I do not regret it. I have found that holding on to things, although it is my natural reaction, never helps – even if we are truly getting the bad deal in a given situation. Giving, releasing and blessing others is the way of the Spirit, and when we choose that path we never lose out in the long-term.

Partnering Those who Are Different from Us

The city of Harare is not an easy place in which to live and work. Over recent years it has been particularly painful to see people's trauma and suffering in a situation that was completely avoidable. It is even more painful, of course, for those who live there. In that context Oasis runs a project among street girls that focuses on rehabilitation and reintegration. One great thing about the approach to street children in Harare is that it is a collaborative effort by several organizations. They work together to provide a continuum of intervention that means girls really can be helped in the multitude of ways necessary for transformation to take place.

Let me tell you about Carol. She grew up in Zimbabwe in an unstable and turbulent home environment. She lived with her stepfather, who she originally thought was her real father, and her mother, who often took out her anger on Carol. Eventually Carol left home and, for a year and a half, she lived on the streets of Harare – in constant danger from other street children and under threat of being placed in a detention centre by the police. In May 2004 she joined the Oasis medium-term rehabilitation programme, but when she discovered she was pregnant she decided to leave and go back to the streets. Oasis was able to connect her to another organization working in the vicinity where she was living. This organization, Streets Ahead, provided her with ongoing practical support. It wasn't easy living on the streets and being pregnant. When it came time for her to give birth, Streets Ahead referred her on to Shelter Trust. They provided a clean and safe environment in which she could give birth. On 2 January 2005, Carol gave birth to beautiful twin girls. Eventually Carol rejoined the Oasis programme and today, at a time when Zimbabwe's unemployment rate stands at nearly 80%, she has been able to secure full-time employment. Carol would probably have fallen through the cracks if these different organizations had not proactively cooperated to meet her needs in specific ways at specific times in her journey to wholeness.

One of the questions people often ask is whether we can effectively partner with those who don't share our values. Lurking behind such questions is often an unexpressed fear – a fear that others will water down our values and ethos. This is not a small issue. The history of the church, certainly in parts of the Western world over the past fifty years, is a history of retreating and working alone for fear of how others will affect us. The saddest thing about this is that it causes us to lose our ability to relate and then we forget that the mosaic God is creating is so much bigger than what 'Christians' are doing. Yes, governments and those of other religious persuasions sometimes do get it right – they do bring justice, compassionate care and blessing to those who are marginalized. They can be God's instruments of transformation even if their values and beliefs are different from our own. As Jean-Paul Heldt said when he reflected on the end of both the Cold War and the scourge of apartheid,

> My inclination is to conclude that God was using Gorbachev and de Klerk, and is still using the International Red Cross, Greenpeace, and Amnesty International in accomplishing God's purposes, in places and circumstances where Christian believers and churches have been silent and supporting the status quo.[9]

Pete Brierley, who oversaw the youth work at the Oasis church in Waterloo, London, told me that, while the churches in the area found it impossible to effectively work together, the secular agencies were very happy to partner together and with him. Not only did they borrow each other's equipment when needed, but they also became involved in joint planning, writing funding bids together, and delivering services in an integrated way. Those who did not share Pete's faith welcomed him as a fellow youth worker and never sought to secularize the agenda he had, which was to see young people reconnected with God.

A meeting was held a few years ago in Bangalore to think through the issue of missing children in the city. The result of that meeting was a request from the Bangalore police for Oasis to partner with them to address this issue. During 2006 there were 2,056 reported cases of missing children. There were just too many cases, and police resources were too limited to follow up on all the cases reported. Oasis staff first wrote some software that would integrate the information about both missing and found children across the 79 police stations in the city. Once the software was finalized and the existing information was entered from all those locations, it was possible to close over 1,150 of the existing cases. Our partnership with the police enabled us to lay the groundwork for a preventative approach to the issues of trafficking that we saw in Chapter 12. As this one example illustrates, partnership with others who share our goals and objectives, regardless of their faith persuasion, is both possible and, in many situations, desirable.

In his book *Kingdom Come* Malcolm Duncan gives an overview of the options that Christians face as they consider partnering with others. After exploring the options of remaining separate or being assimilated, Duncan suggests that Christians can partner with those of other faiths while maintaining the distinctiveness of their own. 'We need a distinctive approach that is theologically grounded, externally accountable and measurably pragmatic.'[10] The Faithworks charter was developed to provide a framework for how this can be done.[11]

It can sometimes be more difficult to partner with those who consider themselves more closely aligned to our ethos and values than it is to partner with those who are clearly different. Issues can arise in relation to both ownership and reputation. One Oasis partnership which didn't work out well, but from which we learned many lessons, was in relation to a small slum community quite central to the city of Mumbai. A church was already involved in that community and touching people's lives. The pastor wanted to develop a more holistic approach, and we came alongside to help in that regard. We shared their values, as well as their desire to see the community transformed. We worked together for several years, but there was an ongoing battle regarding what we owned and what they owned in regard to the work. Again, much of the unease felt on both sides was due to the fact that we did not clearly articulate the nature of the partnership from day one. We also hired staff from that community who attended the church as well – and so they were unsure to whom they were accountable for what. Clarity is an essential ingredient of good partnerships. Although we were naïve in the beginning, we learned our lesson quickly. Even among Christians, this kind of clear and careful documentation is essential.

Building for the Future

Tom Wright, in his book *Surprised by Hope*, argues strongly for God's redemptive approach to the earth. God will renew this world, he says, and not dump it and start all over again. And because of that, Wright argues, all that we do today has incredible value and lasting significance.

> It has often been observed that the robust Jewish and Christian doctrine of resurrection, as part of God's new creation, gives more value, not less, to the present world, and to our present bodies. What these doctrines give, both in classic Judaism and in classic Christianity, is a sense of

continuity between the present world (and the present state) and the future, whatever it shall be, with the result that what we do in the present is seen to matter enormously.[12]

There are some wonderful pictures in Scripture of people living in community and peace that give hope to those who are downtrodden, excluded and suffering injustice. Zechariah paints a picture of Jerusalem in which the young are able to play with abandon while the elderly sit and watch with pleasure.[13] Such scriptural pictures motivate us to apply a redemptive approach to the lives of the broken and to the context in which the poor live and work. Each time we witness redemption in an area of a person's life it is not only a sign of the future, when the whole earth will be redeemed, but it is also a declaration to the world that this future redemption is certainly going to come. For those of us who work among the poor, the knowledge that our work today has lasting value within God's purposes brings great hope and fuels our perseverance. Again, as Tom Wright says, 'What we do in the Lord is "not in vain"; and that is the mandate we need for every act of justice and mercy, every programme of ecology, every effort to reflect God's wise stewardly image into his creation.'[14]

Building on the Work of Others

There is yet another perspective that I believe is important for us to have in our work – and that is an understanding that we are building on the work of others. In any city or community there are almost always others who have gone before and paved the way. Often we don't know who they are or what they have done, but occasionally it will become clear to us that our reaping is because others, often unknown to us, have sown. In our organizations it is good to remind staff that the work most of us do is built on the work that others have done before us. All of us are at some time tempted to see history as beginning when we entered the scene, but the truth is that we all build on the work of other people.

It is also good to remind ourselves that the labels we use now will have no meaning one day. Methodist, Presbyterian, Baptist, Campus Crusade, Teen Challenge, Oasis, YFC, and YWAM are all human labels that have some relevance now only to identify groups of people. In God's great design he has allowed groups to emerge around different visions within the church, but these are temporary and serve a purpose only for a limited time. They are not eternal. Because he understood the life cycle of mission organizations, when Steve Chalke founded Oasis he tried to put in its memorandum that after fifty years the organization would disband, irrespective of how it was doing at the time, and transfer its assets to someone who had a new vision. The founding trustees didn't agree to do this, but it would have been very interesting if they had.

Because all people are made in the image of God, all people are equally precious in his sight. Sin has not simply separated people from him, it has prevented them from being all that God intends. God is at work in the world to see his image fully restored in people. He uses a whole variety of means to achieve this, including among people who do not acknowledge his existence or purposes. As we work to see God's image restored among the poor we do not do so in isolation but as part of the wonderful mosaic of God's work in the world.

14

The Onward Journey

*What I believe is not what I say I believe; what I believe is
what I do.*

– Donald Miller[1]

Most of us reading this book will encounter the poor
today. Perhaps we won't meet street children, or girls
who have been trafficked into prostitution – though they
may live closer to us than we think. But we will meet
people who are marginalized, rejected and oppressed,
who are not part of a community, who are in a trap that
they cannot escape unless someone steps in to help
them, who cannot make choices because opportunity has
been taken away from them. As you encounter those
people today, I hope that first and foremost you see them
as precious people whose dignity must be preserved. I
hope that you see them as people of capacity, not deficiency. I hope you see them as individuals who have
much to offer you – not just as people who might benefit from you. I hope that you see them as whole people
who need to be empowered in all areas of their lives. I
hope you see them as made in God's image.

I hope, too, that you will choose to enter their world,
to walk in their shoes and to share their pain. For as you

do this you follow the one who came to bring good news to the poor; the one who came to proclaim freedom to those who are imprisoned; the one who sought to bring sight to the blind; the one who came to release the oppressed. In reaching out to the poor you follow Christ. And in following Christ you share his pain for our broken world. Don't let the immensity of the task or the numbers of people in need overwhelm or distract you. Focus on the ones and the twos. This is where it begins. And, when you do this, don't be surprised if God takes your five small loaves and two small fishes[2] and creates something that will impact a lot more people than you ever imagined. I am not suggesting you think about the wider implications, however, for you must focus on the few. Leave the rest to God, who often takes the small things and makes something of them that is beyond our wildest dreams.

It is the most amazing experience to walk with someone who has been ostracized, marginalized and oppressed as they come to understand that they have been made in God's image. Instead of viewing themselves as worthless, they begin to see themselves as the pinnacle of God's wonderful creation – for that is truly what they are, what you are, what all of us are. For the awesomeness of creation, rather than the fall, is always our starting point among the poor.

Not long ago Oasis produced a little DVD about two children. One of them was a twelve-year-old boy called Kiran who lived on a railway station in Mumbai. When he became involved in the day centre programme we ran near that station he, of course, came off the streets, started going to school and spent his nights in a shelter we had also set up for boys like him. That was the point of the DVD – to show the difference in these boys' lives that our work was making. We even took him, with the cameras, back to the station. On the DVD he points to the place where he used to live. The climax comes at the very end of the DVD, when he explains that all of this change is because of what Jesus has done in his life and that his vision for the future includes wanting to be an electrician. It is a powerful story, and I have seen people cry while watching it. The trouble is, the story didn't end there. Not long after the footage was shot, Kiran dropped out of school. He then went back to the streets. It was difficult to show the DVD to people, knowing that the example of change we were showing had been overtaken by events and that things were not now as they were portrayed on the film. But that was not the end of the story either.

In the midst of writing this final piece I decided to phone India to find out the latest on Kiran's story. I spoke to Jane, one of our staff members there, literally a minute ago. She told me that she is still in touch with Kiran. He has come off the streets again, gone through a detoxification programme and is back in school. He has become very keen on football. Kiran's story is unfinished. It is a journey, and we choose to walk alongside him on his journey.

For those of you who are involved with people, much of what I have written might resonate in your own heart – I hope it does. For those of you who are thinking of getting involved, why not look up what is going on in your local area? Perhaps there is a programme being run among the homeless or a contact centre for refugees. Maybe there is a debt counselling service that needs volunteers or a day centre for the elderly. All of those are happening in my local area, and all of them welcome volunteer involvement. There are probably similar programmes in your vicinity. It's always best to get started by taking a small step and plugging into something that is already up and running.

The lessons learnt through the stories I have told are hard-earned – they aren't the kind of things you learn from reading a book. So this book may help you as you engage among the poor. It may prepare you for what you might encounter. I hope it will inspire you to engagement if you are not already engaged, but it won't teach you what you need to know. For that, you have to get involved yourself. And as you do that, as you extend your hand and your heart to the poor of this world – you will learn and you will be changed. In fact, you will never be the same again. And you will never regret it.

If you are generous with the hungry
  and start giving yourselves to the down-and-out,
Your lives will begin to glow in the darkness,
  your shadowed lives will be bathed in sunlight.
I will always show you where to go.
I'll give you a full life in the emptiest of places -
  firm muscles, strong bones.
You'll be like a well-watered garden,
  a gurgling spring that never runs dry.[3]

About Oasis

Founded in 1985 by Steve Chalke, Oasis now works in ten countries around the world.

As an organization, Oasis seeks to play its part alongside others in the transformation of local communities as well as reaching the poorest of the poor who have often been excluded from community.

Oasis does this through walking alongside the poor and excluded, empowering people to find their voice, address injustice, and strengthen communities. Oasis works in an integrated and comprehensive way.

For more information log on to www.oasisglobal.org.

Endnotes

Introduction

[1] Please note names have been changed throughout to protect identities of those among whom we are privileged to work.

1 Made in God's Image

[1] Chick Yuill, et al., *The Insistent Challenge to a Reluctant Church* (Milton Keynes: Authentic, 2007), p. 13.
[2] In *Created in God's Image* (Grand Rapids: Eerdmans, 1986) Anthony Hoekema says, 'In fact, the very greatness of man's sin consists in the fact that he is still an image-bearer of God' (p. 85).
[3] James 2:5.
[4] Romans 3:23.
[5] Matthew 6:26.
[6] For both an historical overview and a theological summary see Hoekema, *Created in God's Image*, chs. 4 and 5.
[7] Derek Kidner, *Genesis* (Downers Grove: InterVarsity Press, 1967), p. 51.
[8] Ray Anderson, *On Being Human: Essays in Theological Anthropology* (Grand Rapids: Eerdmans, 1982), p. 84.

9 Chris Wright, *Old Testament Ethics for the People of God* (Milton Keynes: Authentic, 2004), p. 119.

10 G.C. Berkouwer discusses how an approach that differentiated between man's 'higher' and 'lower' qualities created this dualism. He concludes that it is right to think of God's image being inherent in both body and soul (*Man: The Image of God*, pp. 74–77).

11 Anderson, *On Being Human*, p. 72.

12 Anderson, *On Being Human*, p. 72.

13 Gerhard von Rad, *Genesis* (Old Testament Library, London: SCM Press, 1956), p. 56.

14 In *On Being Human* (pp. 70–73), Ray Anderson says that the view that the image of God is limited to a person's soul leads ultimately to an understanding that redemption is about being 'saved out of the world' – rather than redemption being a transformative understanding of God's engagement with the whole of life.

15 Chris Wright, *The Mission of God* (Nottingham: IVP, 2006), p. 429.

16 Berkouwer, *Man: The Image of God*, p. 189.

17 Alan Richardson, *Genesis 1–11: The Creation Stories and the Modern World View* (London: SCM Press, 1953), p. 54.

18 Genesis 9:6.

19 Hoekema, *Created in God's Image*, p. 15.

20 Anderson, *On Being Human*, p. 74.

21 Doug Baker, *Covenant and Community: Our Role as the Image of God* (Eugene, OR: Wipf & Stock, 2008), p. 61.

22 For a full discussion of this issue see Baker, *Covenant and Community*, pp. 60–70.

23 The quotation is from Doug Baker, *Covenant and Community*, p. 75, but his whole book is built around this thesis, which he argues from other angles in addition to the linguistic one. He sees Gen. 1:26 in an eschatological framework.

24 Hoekema, *Created in God's Image*, p. 69.

25 Colossians 3:9–10.
26 Berkouwer, *Man: The Image of God*, p. 99.

2 Understanding Poverty

1 *Walking with the Poor* (New York: Orbis, 1999), p. 86.
2 Genesis 1:28–30.
3 For a full discussion of this see Chris Wright, *Old Testament Ethics*, ch. 4, 'Ecology and the Earth'. Also see 'A Rocha', an organization specifically set up to help people understand what the Bible says about creation care – (http://www.arocha.org).
4 Dewi Hughes, *God of the Poor: A Biblical Vision of God's Present Rule* (Carlisle: OM Publishing, 1998), p. 157.
5 http://www.globalissues.org/print/article/26.
6 Leviticus 25:23.
7 Leviticus 25:11–13.
8 Leviticus 25:36.
9 Leviticus 25:39.
10 Hughes, *God of the Poor*, p. 157.
11 Steve Chalke and Alan Mann, *The Lost Message of Jesus* (Grand Rapids: Zondervan, 2004), p. 96.
12 Myers, *Walking with the Poor*, p. 86.
13 Kenneth Bailey covers the whole episode recorded in Luke 7:36–50 in *Through Peasant Eyes* (Grand Rapids: Eerdmans, 1980), ch. 1.
14 The first time I heard this distinction was from Ivan Raskino, a pastor in Mumbai who taught me much.
15 This is found in two places – Matthew 26:11 and John 12:8. Both passages record the same incident from the last week of Jesus' life.
16 This is taken from the passage in John (12:5). In Matthew's version the words are attributed to the disciples rather than directly to Judas.

[17] Deuteronomy 15:11.

[18] Brian McLaren, *Everything Must Change: Jesus, Global Crises, and a Revolution of Hope* (Nashville: Thomas Nelson, 2007), p. 121.

[19] Jim Wallis, *God's Politics* (Oxford: Lion, 2005), p. 209.

[20] Wallis, *God's Politics*, p. 210.

[21] John 13:29.

[22] Esteban Voth, in R. Padilla, et al., *The Local Church, Agent of Transformation: An Ecclesiology for Integral Mission*, discusses various understandings of the encounter which Jesus had with this woman who anointed him (pp. 51–54).

3 Community

[1] Donald Miller, *Blue Like Jazz* (Nashville: Thomas Nelson, 2003), p. 154.

[2] Henri Nouwen, *In the House of the Lord: The Journey from Fear to Love* (London: Darton, Longman & Todd, 1986), p. 14.

[3] His name has been changed to protect his identity.

[4] Matthew Frost, 'The Burning Question', *Faithworks Magazine* (Autumn 2007), p. 9.

[5] 'Your Poverty Is Greater than Ours', *Journal Chrétien* (25 Aug. 2007), http://journalchretien.net/spip.php?breve349.

[6] Genesis 1:26.

[7] John Calvin, *A Commentary on Genesis* (translated from the Latin in 1847; Edinburgh: Banner of Truth, 1965), p. 91.

[8] John 14:31.

[9] Matthew 11:27.

[10] John 10:30.

[11] Genesis 2:18.

[12] Baker, *Covenant and Community*, p. 101.

[13] Myers, *Walking with the Poor*, p. 43.

[14] Wright, *The Mission of God*, p. 427.

[15] See a chapter written by Samuel Escobar on the church as community in Padilla, Voth, et al., *The Local Church*, p. 139.

16 See John's wonderful introduction to his recording of the events of Jesus' life in John 1.
17 Rob Bell, *Velvet Elvis: Repainting the Christian Faith* (Grand Rapids: Zondervan, 2006), pp. 129–34.
18 Mark 5:30.
19 Bell, *Velvet Elvis*, p. 107.
20 Myers, *Walking with the Poor*, p. 150.
21 Michael Schluter, 'What Charter for Humanity? Defining the Destination of Development', *Cambridge Papers* 15 (3) 2006, pp.1–4 (1). For a fuller understanding of the connection between relationships and well-being see *The R Factor* by Schluter and David Lee (London: Hodder & Stoughton, 1993).

4 Wholeness

1 'Revisiting the "Whole Gospel": Toward a Biblical Model of Holistic Mission in the Twenty-first Century,' *Missiology* 32.2 (2004), pp. 149–72 (162).
2 This was a UN statistic in the mid-1990s. Nobody really knows the exact number, and all global figures are estimates. See http://www.180degreesalliance.org/faqs.htm#2.
There are many examples of this. The following website mentions a few of them:
http://www.180degreesalliance.org/faqs.htm#2.
3 http://www.180degreesalliance.org/faqs.htm#2.
4 Issues of risk and personal safety are always complex and, when facing these dilemmas, there are no easy answers. In the particular situations we encountered we made the best choices we could with the information that we had available.
5 See Thomas McAlpine, *By Word, Work and Wonder: Cases in Holistic Mission* (Monrovia: MARC, 1995), ch. 1, for background on the use of the term 'holism'.

[6] See McAlpine, *By Word, Work and Wonder*, for case studies and a discussion on how these three elements interrelate.

[7] This occurred at a strategy meeting of 180 Degree Alliance, which brings together a number of different organizations working among street children. The focus is on helping the thousands of small projects around the world that don't have the resources or knowledge of the larger organizations. This particular meeting was held in October 2006 in Cape Town, South Africa.

[8] Wright, *The Mission of God*, ch. 9.

[9] David Bosch, *Transforming Mission: Paradigm Shifts in Theology of Mission* (American Society of Missiology Series 16; New York: Orbis, 1991), p. 401.

[10] Bosch, *Transforming Mission*, p. 399.

[11] Malcolm Duncan, *Kingdom Come: The Local Church as a Catalyst for Social Change* (Oxford: Monarch, 2007), p. 206. Duncan goes on to reference Matthew 22:37–40 and the inseparability of loving God and loving our neighbour.

[12] Myers, *Walking with the Poor*, p. 6.

[13] Berkouwer, *Man: The Image of God*, p. 77.

[14] Matthew 14:16.

[15] Baker, *Covenant and Community*, p. 67.

[16] Hoekema, *Created in God's Image*, p. 216.

[17] Myers, *Walking with the Poor*, p. 135.

[18] Ray Bakke, *A Theology as Big as the City* (Downers Grove: InterVarsity Press, 1997), pp. 8-19.

5 Change

[1] Philip Yancey, *The Jesus I Never Knew* (London: Marshall Pickering, 1995), p. 76.

[2] Berkouwer, *Man: The Image of God*, p. 320.

[3] Clare Nonhebel, *Finding Oasis* (Milton Keynes: Authentic, 2010).

4 Matthew 9:1–8.

5 Nouwen, *In the House of the Lord*, p. 44.

6 Brian McLaren, The Secret Message of Jesus (Nashville: Thomas Nelson, 2006), p. 48.

7 Matthew 9:2.

8 John 3:1–21.

9 John 4:4–26.

10 Yancey, *The Jesus I Never Knew*, p. 76.

11 Yancey, *The Jesus I Never Knew*, p. 78.

6 Empowerment

1 'Development: A Term in Need of Transformation', *Evangelical Missions Quarterly* 42.1 (Jan. 2006), pp. 52–58 (57).

2 Ernesto Sirolli, *Ripples from the Zambezi* (Gabriola Island: New Society Publishers, 1999), p. 1.

3 William Easterly, *The White Man's Burden* (Oxford: Oxford University Press, 2007).

4 Robert Lupton, *Theirs Is the Kingdom: Celebrating the Gospel in Urban America* (New York: HarperSanFrancisco, 1989), p. 72.

5 Starcher, 'Development', p. 56.

6 Leviticus 19:9ff.

7 Padilla, Voth, et al., The Local Church, p. 59.

8 Exodus 23:10–11.

9 Hughes, *God of the Poor*, p. 158.

10 John McKnight, *The Careless Society: Community and Its Counterfeits* (New York: Basic Books, 1996), pp. 28ff.

11 Myers, *Walking with the Poor*, p. 66.

12 Again, John McKnight, in his book *The Careless Society*, uses the term 'client-provider'. Shane Claiborne relates this to the church and to the faith-based non-profit context in *The Irresistible Revolution: Living as an Ordinary Radical* (Grand

Rapids: Zondervan, 2006). Claiborne says that if this focus directs the way we work, then the rich never face the poor and so power does not shift. He contrasts this system of 'brokerage' with what the church should be as community.

[13] Myers, *Walking with the Poor*, pp. 115-16.

[14] Craig Greenfield, *The Urban Halo* (Milton Keynes: Authentic, 2007).

[15] Chalke and Mann, *The Lost Message of Jesus*, p. 67.

7 Compassion

[1] See   http://womenshistory.about.com/od/quotes/a/mother_teresa.htm.

[2] If you want to find these, a good place to begin is to assess progress against the UN's Millennium Development Goals (http://www.un.org/millenniumgoals/).

[3] Gary Haugen, *Good News about Injustice: A Witness of Courage in a Hurting World* (Downers Grove: InterVarsity Press, 1999), p. 79.

[4] Haugen, *Good News about Injustice*, p. 80.

[5] Charles Van Engen and Jude Tiersma (eds.), *God So Loves the City: Seeking a Theology for Urban Mission* (Monrovia: MARC, 1994), p. 14.

[6] Lupton, *Theirs Is the Kingdom*, p. 18.

[7] Jackie Pullinger, speaking at a conference in Secunderabad, India in 1996.

[8] Mark 1:41.

[9] Luke 7:11–15.

[10] Mark 8:22–25.

[11] Matthew 9:36.

[12] Matthew 14:15–21; 15:29–38.

[13] Luke 13:34.

[14] Luke 19:41.

[15] John 8:28–29; 14:10; 15:15.

[16] Dewi Hughes and Matthew Bennett, in section 1 of their book *God of the Poor*, place engagement among the poor in the world, both at an individual and macro-level, within the context of the kingdom of God. Malcolm Duncan's book Kingdom Come also places local church community engagement within the framework of the kingdom. Duncan gives plenty of examples of how the principles he articulates can be effectively put into action.

[17] Duncan, *Kingdom Come*, p. 190.

[18] John 10:10.

[19] Mary Thiesen in Van Engen and Tiersma (eds.), *God so Loves the City*, p. 83.

8 Justice

[1] Rob Bell and Don Golden, *Jesus Wants to Save Christians* (Grand Rapids: Zondervan, 2008), p. 163.

[2] Mark Labberton, *The Dangerous Act of Worship: Living God's Call to Justice* (Downers Grove: InterVarsity Press, 2007), p. 25.

[3] Isaiah 58 is probably the most well-known example of this. The prophet contrasted their days of fasting when they exploited their workers with true fasting, which is about loosing the chains of injustice and setting oppressed people free.

[4] Labberton, *The Dangerous Act of Worship*, p. 21.

[5] Steve Chalke and Simon Johnston, *Intimacy and Involvement* (Eastbourne: Kingsway, 2003).

[6] Leviticus 25.

[7] Leviticus 25:23–24.

[8] Padilla, Voth, et al., *The Local Church*, p. 97.

[9] Quote from Dr Jonathan Ingleby, Dr Cathy Ross, and J.V. Taylor, 'Shouting above the Storm: Speaking out about Injustice' (Global Connections conference, 2007).

[10] Paul Hertig, 'The Jubilee Mission of Jesus in the Gospel of Luke: Reversals of Fortunes, *Missiology* 26.2 (1998), pp. 167–79 (176).

[11] Matthew 23:23.

[12] Matthew 25:31–46.

9 Prayer

[1] *Nothing but a Thief: The Street and Her Children* (Tonbridge: Sovereign World, 2002), p. 180.

[2] Clare Nonhebel, *Far from Home: Stories of the Homeless and the Search for the Heart's True Home* (Oxford: Lion, 1999), p. 15.

[3] Romans 1:20.

[4] This particular redemptive analogy, recorded in Richardson's book *Peace Child* (Ventura, CA: Regal, 1974), was the exchange of children between two villages in order to make peace between them.

[5] Myers, *Walking with the Poor*, p. 117.

[6] Acts 10:34–35.

[7] At a conference in Hyderabad, India in January 1996.

[8] You can read her story in *Chasing the Dragon* (London: Hodder, 1980).

[9] 1 John 4:10.

[10] Luke 5:12–13.

[11] The best book I have read on this topic is Pete Greig's *God on Mute: Engaging the Silence of Unanswered Prayer*, which deals with this issue in detail (Eastbourne: Kingsway, 2007).

[12] Matthew 6:11.

[13] Luke 18:9–14.

[14] Bailey, *Through Peasant Eyes*, ch. 9.

10 Receiving

[1] *In the Name of Jesus: Reflections on Christian Leadership* (New York: Crossroad, 1989), p. 48.

2 Labberton, *The Dangerous Act of Worship*, pp. 159–60.

3 Claiborne, *The Irresistible Revolution*, p. 51.

4 Nouwen, *In the Name of Jesus*, p. 57. Nouwen gave up his prestigious professorship at Yale and moved to L'Arche community to work among the mentally challenged.

5 James 2:5.

6 2 Corinthians 8:1–4.

7 Luke 21:1–4.

8 Nouwen, *In the House of the Lord*, p. 29.

9 Acts 20:35.

11 Celebration

1 At a conference in Mumbai in August 1993.

2 Claiborne, *The Irresistible Revolution*, p. 188.

3 Unfortunately, because the event had to be rescheduled, I was in Australia on the day of the show. The staff were able to record it so I could watch it when I returned.

4 Eugene Peterson, *The Message* (Colorado Springs: NavPress, 2004), p. 1410. Based on Luke 7:31–35.

5 Luke 14:15–24.

6 Bakke, *A Theology as Big as the City*, p. 12.

12 Prevention

1 *Good News about Injustice*, p. 144.

2 Myers, *Walking with the Poor*, p. 123.

3 Wallis, *God's Politics*, p. 236.

4 Wallis, *God's Politics*, p. 240.

5 www.stopthetraffik.org, quoted from *Bitter Chocolate: The Dark Side of the World's Most Seductive Sweet* by Carol Off (New York: The New Press, 2008).

13 Perspective

1 *Building a Better World: Faith at Work for Change in Society* (London: Continuum, 2006), p. 139.
2 Patrick McDonald with Emma Garrow, *Reaching Children in Need: What's Being Done – What You Can Do* (Eastbourne: Kingsway, 2000), p. 78–79.
3 Some translations of the Bible have 70 and some 72.
4 Mark 9:38 and Luke 9:49.
5 Luke 9:50.
6 John 17:21.
7 1 Corinthians 1:2.
8 Romans 1:7.
9 Heldt, 'Revisiting the "Whole Gospel"', p. 160.
10 Duncan, *Kingdom Come*, p. 116.
11 The Faithworks charter can be obtained on their website (www.faithworks.info).
12 Tom Wright, *Surprised by Hope* (London: SPCK, 2007), p. 37.
13 Zechariah 8:4–5.
14 Wright, *Surprised by Hope*, p. 221.

14 The Onward Journey

1 *Blue Like Jazz*, p. 110.
2 See John 6:8–9.
3 Peterson, *The Message*, p. 993, Isaiah 58:10–11.

Bibliography

Anderson, R., *On Being Human: Essays in Theological Anthropology* (Grand Rapids: Eerdmans, 1982).

Bailey, K., *Poet and Peasant and Through Peasant Eyes* (Grand Rapids: Eerdmans, 1980).

Baker, D., *Covenant and Community: Our Role as the Image of God* (Eugene, OR: Wipf & Stock, 2008).

Bakke, R., *A Theology as Big as the City* (Downers Grove: InterVarsity Press, 1997).

Bell, R., *Velvet Elvis: Repainting the Christian Faith* (Grand Rapids: Zondervan, 2006).

Bell, R., and D. Golden., *Jesus Wants to Save Christians* (Grand Rapids: Zondervan, 2008).

Berkouwer, G.C., *Studies in Dogmatics – Man: The Image of God* (Grand Rapids: Eerdmans, 1962).

Bosch, D., *Transforming Mission: Paradigm Shifts in Theology of Mission* (American Society of Missiology Series 16; New York: Orbis, 1991).

Calvin, J., *A Commentary on Genesis* (translated from the Latin in 1847; Edinburgh: Banner of Truth, 1965).

Campolo, T., *Revolution and Renewal: How Churches Are Saving our Cities* (Louisville: Westminster John Knox Press, 2000).

Chalke, S., and A. Mann., *The Lost Message of Jesus* (Grand Rapids: Zondervan, 2004).

Chalke, S., and S. Johnston., *Intimacy and Involvement* (Eastbourne: Kingsway, 2003).

Claiborne, S., *The Irresistible Revolution: Living as an Ordinary Radical* (Grand Rapids: Zondervan, 2006).

Cosden, D., *The Heavenly Good of Earthly Work* (Milton Keynes: Paternoster; Peabody, MA: Hendrickson, 2006).

Duncan, M., *Building a Better World: Faith at Work for Change in Society* (London: Continuum, 2006).

—, *Kingdom Come: The Local Church as a Catalyst for Social Change* (Oxford: Monarch, 2007).

Easterly, W., *The White Man's Burden* (Oxford: Oxford University Press, 2007).

Greenfield, C., *The Urban Halo* (Milton Keynes: Authentic, 2007).

Greig, P., *God on Mute: Engaging the Silence of Unanswered Prayer* (Eastbourne: Kingsway, 2007).

Grigg, V., *Cry of the Urban Poor: Reaching the Slums of Today's Megacities* (Milton Keynes: Authentic and World Vision, 2005).

Haugen, G.A., *Good News about Injustice: A Witness of Courage in a Hurting World* (Downers Grove: InterVarsity Press, 1999).

Heldt, J.P., 'Revisiting the "Whole Gospel": Toward a Biblical Model of Holistic Mission in the Twenty-first Century', *Missiology* 32.2 (2004), pp. 149–72.

Hertig, P., 'The Jubilee Mission of Jesus in the Gospel of Luke: Reversals of Fortunes', *Missiology* 26.2 (1998), pp. 167–9.

Hoekema, A., *Created in God's Image* (Grand Rapids: Eerdmans; Exeter: Paternoster, 1986).

Hughes, D., with M. Bennett., *God of the Poor: A Biblical Vision of God's Present Rule* (Carlisle: OM Publishing, 1998).

Kidner, D., *Genesis* (Downers Grove: InterVarsity Press, 1967).

Labberton, M., *The Dangerous Act of Worship: Living God's Call to Justice* (Downers Grove: InterVarsity Press, 2007).

Linthicum, R.C., *Empowering the Poor: Community Organizing among the City's 'Rag, Tag and Bobtail'* (Monrovia: MARC, 1991).

Lupton, R., *Theirs Is the Kingdom: Celebrating the Gospel in Urban America* (New York: HarperSanFrancisco, 1989).

McAlpine, T.H., *By Word, Work and Wonder: Cases in Holistic Mission* (Monrovia: MARC, 1995).

McDonald, P., with E. Garrow., *Reaching Children in Need* (Eastbourne: Kingsway, 2000).

McKnight, J., *The Careless Society: Community and Its Counterfeits* (New York: Basic Books, 1996).

McLaren, B., *The Secret Message of Jesus* (Nashville: Thomas Nelson, 2006).

—, *Everything Must Change: Jesus, Global Crises, and a Revolution of Hope* (Nashville: Thomas Nelson, 2007).

Miller, D., *Blue Like Jazz* (Nashville: Thomas Nelson, 2003).

Murray, S., *The Challenge of the City: A Biblical Overview* (Tonbridge: Sovereign World, 1993).

Myers, B., *Walking with the Poor* (New York: Orbis, 1999).

Nonhebel, C., *Far from Home: Stories of the Homeless and the Search for the Heart's True Home* (Oxford: Lion, 1999).

—, *Finding Oasis* (Milton Keynes: Authentic, 2010).

Nouwen, H., *In the House of the Lord: The Journey from Fear to Love* (London: Darton, Longman & Todd, 1986).

—, *In the Name of Jesus: Reflections on Christian Leadership* (New York: Crossroad, 1989).

Off, C., *Bitter Chocolate: The Dark Side of the World's Most Seductive Sweet* (New York: The New Press, 2008).

Padilla, R., T. Yamamori, et al., *The Local Church, Agent of Transformation: An Ecclesiology for Integral Mission* (Buenos Aires: Ediciones Kairos, 2004).

Perkins, J.M., *Restoring At-Risk Communities: Doing it Together and Doing it Right* (Grand Rapids: Baker Books, 1995).

Peterson, E., *The Message* (Colorado Springs: NavPress, 2004).

Pullinger, J., *Chasing the Dragon* (London: Hodder, 1980).

Richardson, D., *Peace Child* (Ventura, CA: Regal, 1974).

Richardson, A., *Genesis 1–11: The Creation Stories and the Modern World View* (London: SCM Press, 1953).

Schluter, M., 'What Charter for Humanity? Defining the Destination of Development', *Cambridge Papers* 15 (3) 2006, pp.1-4.

Schluter, M., and D. Lee., *The R Factor* (London: Hodder & Stoughton, 1993).

Sirolli, E., *Ripples from the Zambezi* (Gabriola Island: New Society Publishers, 1999).

Starcher, R., 'Development: A Term in Need of Transformation', *Evangelical Missions Quarterly* 42 (1) 2006, pp. 52-58.

Speakman, D., *Nothing but a Thief: The Street and Her Children* (Tonbridge: Sovereign World, 2002).

von Rad, G., *Genesis* (Old Testament Library; London: SCM Press, 1956).

Van Engen, C., and J. Tiersma (eds.), *God So Loves the City: Seeking a Theology for Urban Mission* (Monrovia: MARC, 1994).

Wallis, J., *God's Politics* (Oxford: Lion, 2005).

Wright, C., *The Mission of God* (Nottingham: IVP, 2006).

Wright, C., *Old Testament Ethics for the People of God* (Milton Keynes: Authentic, 2004).

Wright, T., *Surprised by Hope* (London: SPCK, 2007).

Yamamori, T., B.L. Myers, and D. Conner., *Serving with the Poor in Asia: Cases in Holistic Ministry* (Monrovia: MARC, 1995).

Yancey, P., *The Jesus I Never Knew* (London: Marshall Pickering, 1995).

Yuill, C., et al., *The Insistent Challenge to a Reluctant Church* (Milton Keynes: Authentic, 2007).